Advertising in Contemporary Society

Perspectives
Toward
Understanding

Advertising in Contemporary Society

Perspectives Toward Understanding

Kim B. Rotzoll
Head of the Department of Advertising
University of Illinois at Urbana–Champaign

James E. Haefner
Associate Professor of Advertising
Director of Graduate Studies in Advertising
University of Illinois at Urbana–Champaign

Consulting Author:
Charles H. Sandage
Professor Emeritus of Advertising
University of Illinois at Urbana–Champaign

Published by

S50 SOUTH-WESTERN PUBLISHING CO.

CINCINNATI   WEST CHICAGO, IL   DALLAS   PELHAM MANOR, NY   LIVERMORE, CA

*To Nancy, Keith, Kristy, and Jason
and to my parents with love and thanks*

KBR

*For Margaret, Jason, and Adam
and especially Nick and Martha*

JEH

Contents

Part 2
Issues
of
Consequence

Foreword

Advertising is a paradox. In one sense it is generally unloved. It may be tolerated, but it is rarely championed. It is the source of jokes and the target of them. It reveals more about our selfish, grasping natures than we find comforting to address as often as it relentlessly assures us we must. The public's judgments of its ethical standards place it at or near the bottom of virtually any occupational array, while leading academics savage its social and cultural role.[1] There is also no real shelter under the cloak of expertise. For all of us may realize that we couldn't write an acceptable news story, prescribe a drug, examine an optical system, design a house or bridge, or prepare a legal brief, but we're pretty certain *we* could come up with one of those catchy slogans, clever headlines, or arresting jingles . . .

All of this, of course, sometimes makes it difficult to take advertising seriously. Yet, a recent article in *The Chronicle of Higher Education* carried the headline "Scholars Sold on the Importance of Studying Advertising's History and Role in Society."[2] The author discusses six recent or forthcoming book-length treatments of advertising from communication scholars, historians, and a sociologist. Advertising may be unloved, but it would seem to be at least intriguing.

On a somewhat less lofty plane, the television networks have found

---

1. See Mela Sangha and Richard Pollay, *Advertising's Cultural Impact: A Review of Scholarly Conventional Wisdom*, Working Paper #766 (University of British Columbia: History of Advertising Archives, 1981).

2. "Scholars Sold on the Importance of Studying Advertising's History and Role in Society," *Chronicle of Higher Education*, October 3, 1984.

that entire programs devoted to commercials are at least as popular as much of their prime-time menu. T-shirts and everyday discourse attest to the advertising-spawned influences in our popular culture, and the much-heralded yuppie life-style would seem to embrace advertising's siren call with self-centered abandon. As columnist George Will observed, "A country which has the Great Lakes yet spends zillions for French water in little green bottles is probably ready for designer antifreeze. Are you paying attention, Bill Blass?"

As this brief sampling of diversities suggests, advertising in contemporary society is a crossroad where many interests meet, and, not infrequently, collide. In this book we attempt to offer readers:

1. A basically *deductive* approach to the subject matter.
2. A source that attempts to raise provocative *questions* in a context designed to offer some overall understanding of their implications.
3. A basic *format* for the organization of a college or university level course in the subject area.

When approaching the topics concerned with advertising in contemporary society, there is a great temptation to fill academic hours with discussions of lively topics likely to spur immediate student interest. Such potentially provocative subjects might include children and advertising, sex and advertising, and—the intriguingly elusive—advertising and the "quality of life."

For better or for worse, we have avoided this *ad hoc* avenue of study. We first offer *basic* perspectives (Part 1) that may be fruitfully brought to bear in an attempt to understand advertising, and only then turn our attention to several issues of consequence (Part 2) that seem likely to endure as long as the institution itself.

If there is a prevailing theme to the book, it is simply that how we as individuals *think* about things has a great deal to do with how we act toward them, the kinds of "problems" that we define, as well as what we may consider appropriate "solutions."

Our former colleague Richard Nielsen once offered the tale of the three scholars shipwrecked on a desolate island with but a single can of beans. The chemist suggested, "We can build a fire, place the can in it, and the ensuing molecular activity will cause the can to rupture, thus freeing the contents." The engineer added, "If we constructed an enclosure from indigenous materials, we could contain the contents of the ruptured vessel." Their eyes turned to the economist, who said . . . "Assume we have a can opener."

Basically, the "assumptions" we make about what advertising *is* doing in society, as well as what it *ought* to be doing, are, we believe, crucial to understanding much about the defenses raised, the charges aired, and the practices endorsed or condemned.

In the preparation of this book we are, of course, indebted to many. Vince Norris first exposed Rotzoll to advertising's larger picture during stimulating years at Penn State and has continued to serve as one of advertising's and advertising education's most arresting gadflies. Arnold Barban, now of Texas, suggested the idea of a book based on the structure of the University of Illinois course with the same name.

In the year of this writing, our colleague Charles Sandage has been elected to the Advertising Hall of Fame, the only modern-day educator so honored. It was clearly Sandy's farsighted principles-first approach to advertising education in general, and his Socratic probings in this subject area during his prolific teaching years at Illinois, that provided the true inspiration for this work. His insights, at 82, continue to work their way.

The word processor may have replaced the typewriter, but the effort of preparing a manuscript is still intense. Our thanks to Kathy Mann, Mary Lowrey, and Patti Weisner for that intensity and for their unflagging good spirits when other moods might have seemed more appropriate.

Finally, Rotzoll has had the pleasure of teaching Advertising in Contemporary Society at Illinois for the last 14 years. To all the students from whom I have learned so much, my thanks.

Part 1

Basic
Perspectives

Chapter 1

Introduction: Four Guiding Premises

The late Howard Gossage, member of the Copywriters Hall of Fame and resident critic of the business, once served a stint as Visiting Professor of Advertising at Penn State. Reflecting on the experience, he observed:

> In my lecturing I find I must spend about half my time clearing away the deadwood before I can begin to talk constructively about advertising and what it can do and occasionally does do.[1]

It is an experience shared not only by practitioners, but also by those who seek to examine advertising in anything approaching a dispassionate manner. Putting it simply, advertising in America comes with a great deal of baggage. As we shall attempt to make clear, some of this we carry with us—i.e., we "see with our ideas as well as our eyes," to borrow Walton Hamilton's wonderful phrase[2]—while some is simply inherent in the multilayered structure and workings of the advertising business and its processes.

Owing in part to our (sometimes reluctant) familiarity with its fruits, and in no small part to its apparent simplicity and simplemindedness, advertising lends itself to generalizations. Thus it is easy to fall into statements such as "Advertising does . . ." and "All ads are . . ." Such thinking deadens analysis, cheapening the subject and the observer alike.

The purpose of this chapter is, then, to provide what we consider to be several useful reference points through the forest, while tidying up at least some of the deadwood in the process. These "guiding premises" possess all the strengths and weaknesses of generalities. Yet they do, we have found, explain much. All will be expanded in subsequent chapters.

1. ADVERTISING MUST BE CONSIDERED IN LIGHT OF CUL-
TURAL EXPECTATIONS. Consider the observations of two authors of
important recent books on American advertising—one a historian, the
other a sociologist.

Stephen Fox:
One may build a compelling case that American culture is—beyond
redemption—money mad, hedonistic, superficial, rushing heedlessly
down a railroad track called Progress. De Tocqueville and other observers
of the young republic describe America in these terms in the early 1800s,
decades before the development of national advertising.[3]

Michael Schudson:
We live and shall live, barring nuclear or other disaster, in what has been
called a "promotional" culture. America has long been a nation of sales-
men, and the "shoeshine and a smile" that were Willy Loman's stock-in-
trade are now the tools of politicians and religious evangelists and hospital administrators as much as of advertising agents and public-relations
directors. The promotional culture has worked its way into what we read,
what we care about, the ways we raise our children, our ideas of right and
wrong conduct, our attribution of significance to "image" in both public
and private life. The promotional culture has been celebrated and in-
dulged in. It has been ridiculed and reviled. It still needs to be understood.[4]

Given these deeply rooted values in our society, it is not difficult to
understand how advertising could flourish. Thus, as we will observe in
other chapters, much about advertising in contemporary society can be
better understood by searching for what Hamilton has called "that body
of ideas taken for granted which is called common sense."[5]

In this society these ideas have generally included at least a toleration
(and sometimes admiration) of *persuasion*, based on other well-worn assumptions such as self-interest as a driving force of human action, the
ability of the individual to be "deliberate and calculating" in pursuit of
that self-interest, and the implicit expectation that the self-interested
actions of individuals will ultimately work themselves out to the good of
the whole.

Adam Smith would feel quite at home here, as, apparently, do millions
of our citizens. And these "understandings" that we carry with us have a
strong influence on our perceptions of the world around us, often without conscious thought. First-time visitors to our shores often comment
on the enormous presence of advertising in our mass media, in/around/
above our athletic stadiums, on our clothing, beside our roadways, etc.
For many Americans, however, this is simply "world taken for granted." It
is in line with our "cultural expectations." Throughout this book, then,
we will attempt to examine why that is so, and plumb its implications.

For much of advertising in contemporary society can be understood
with greater clarity if we realize that, as Carey expressed it, "institutions
are the embodiment of ideas."[6] Certainly, then, as the ideas differ so will

the perceptions of the institution. Much can be explained about the defenses and critiques of contemporary advertising thought and practice if we keep this in mind from the outset.

2. THE ADVERTISING PROCESS HAS VARIED INTENTS AND EFFECTS. In addition to the ideas that shape our perceptions of advertising, we must also keep in mind the impressive variety of intentions and effects (many unintended) that characterize its practice. Consider, for example, that while you read these pages, *at least* the following advertising activities are under way:

- PRODUCERS (singly or in association, national or regional) of consumer goods and/or services, advertising to reach individual consumers through radio, television, magazines, newspapers, billboards, direct mail, transit, and other media, to encourage sales of a product or service.
- PRODUCERS (singly or in association, national or regional) of consumer goods and/or services, advertising to reach retailers and wholesalers through trade magazines, newsletters, and direct mail to encourage retailers and wholesalers to stock and/or promote the product or service to *their* customers.
- PRODUCERS (singly or in association, national or regional) of consumer and/or business goods and/or services, advertising to reach individual consumers, government, social institutions, groups, and their own employees through consumer and business print and broadcast media to influence favorable thinking and possible action among key publics concerning *public relations.*
- PRODUCERS (singly or in association) of consumer and/or business goods and/or services, advertising to reach other producers, retailers and wholesalers, governments, social institutions, and groups through business magazines and newsletters, direct mail, and some consumer media to encourage sales for a particular *business* product and/or service for use, and/or recommendation.
- PRODUCERS (singly or in association) of consumer and/or business goods and/or services in *international* distribution, advertising to reach individual consumers, retailers, other businesses, governments, social institutions, and groups through consumer and business media in other countries to encourage specific purchase, to influence key publics, and to foster retail distribution.
- RETAILERS (singly or in association) of goods and/or services, advertising to reach individual consumers through local newspapers, radio, television, magazines, billboards, transit, and direct mail to encourage purchase of particular items and/or services.
- INDIVIDUAL CITIZENS advertising to reach other individuals, primarily through local newspapers (classified), posters, and CATV to encourage purchase of a particular item(s) and/or service.

- GOVERNMENTS, SOCIAL INSTITUTIONS, AND GROUPS advertising to reach individual consumers, government bodies, groups, and
  associations through consumer and specialized media to encourage
  belief in particular practices, to alter behavior in socially desirable
  ways, and to seek political ends, as well as to "sell."[7]

There is much to be learned from this summary, particularly in the
clearing-the-deadwood sense. When we begin to discuss advertising with
others, there is a strong pull to have the common denominator become
television advertising, and that in a rather generic sense. Yet, as we all
know, and the above listing makes clear, there is much more under the
advertising banner. For example, are critics of advertising as concerned
about a *New Yorker* ad for the Great Books Series as they are about a
30-second minidrama promoting a brand of sanitary napkins in late
prime time? Are supporters as willing to defend advertising as the
shopper's best friend when confronted with a jingle for toothpaste rather
than a straightforward list of special price reductions? We can avoid these
traps by avoiding the generalizations that spawn them.

And what of the different *intents*? Some, of course, are obvious on the
surface, but even here brands may have different aspirations in terms of
maintaining awareness, communicating new selling information, reinforcing or attempting to alter attitudes, etc. Then there are the factors
relating advertising to other tools of marketing. Clearly, for example, the
expected contribution of Avon's advertising is quite different than that
of Revlon's. Not infrequently there are also intents that are anything but
transparent to the outside observer. For example, a marketing manager of
a large urban hospital recently confided, "I'm certain that at least two
important groups read our ads—our employees and our competitors. If
the ads do nothing more than influence them they'll have paid their way."
Yet if *we* were asked to assess whether this hospital's advertisements
were "effective," we would probably have invoked criteria other than
those used by the advertiser. Thus to attempt to evaluate an advertisement, it would seem prudent to at least attempt to discern the advertiser's intent. Owing to the presence of myriad agendas—some more apparent than others—even that may not be as simple as we might expect.

Nor, of course, is it simple to predict the individual's *response*. A
headline for a recent advertisement from the American Association of
Advertising Agencies stated, "Isn't it funny how stereo ads are boring
until you want a stereo?" A reasonable point, although far more applica-
ble to media to which we control our exposure (e.g., magazines, newspapers) than to others (e.g., television, billboards). We do, of course, selec-
tively perceive advertisements, as we do other items in our environment.
Howard Gossage frequently observed, "Nobody reads ads *per se*. People
read what interests them, and sometimes it's an ad."[8] One could, for example, hypothesize that as media become more specialized the irritation

factor of advertising will diminish. Thus someone watching a cable sports channel or reading *Golf* magazine may be more likely to find the advertisements of interest than the same individual watching the heterogeneous commercial mix on prime-time network television.

Much can be learned about advertising in contemporary society by realizing that frequently it seeks us out, rather than we it. And our responses to this often unintended encounter can range from surprise, amusement, and interest to irritation, disgust, and apathy. It is, again, a complex reality that wars against simplification.

There is, then, a great deal going on under the advertising umbrella for both the sender and the receiver. To slip into "All advertising . . ." thinking when faced with these nuances throws reason to the winds.

3. ADVERTISING'S ACTUAL EFFECTS ARE USUALLY NOT CLEARLY KNOWN. Commenting on advertising's presumed impact, historian Fox observed:

> Outsiders see only the smooth, expertly contrived finished product, often better crafted than the programming and editorial material it interrupts. Insiders know the messy process of creating an ad, the false starts, rejected ideas, midnight despair, the failures and account losses and creative angst behind any ad that finally appears.[9]

If one were to harbor any illusions about the omnipotence of the advertising process in the hands of steely-eyed technicians of communication, Fox should give us pause, and television critic Michael Arlen's engrossing account of the creative odyssey of a single AT&T advertisement, *Thirty Seconds,*[10] should turn us into card-carrying skeptics. Advertisers are not nearly as powerful as they would like to be. There are, we believe, two central reasons:

a. *It is difficult to determine advertising's effect in relation to other possible influences on the same outcome.* Most advertisers, most of the time, are interested in affecting buying behavior with their messages. But they are also interested in affecting behavior with their pricing strategy, sales promotional efforts, sales force deployment, packaging, and so on. (It is instructive to note that, on the average, overall media advertising represents only about 20 percent of all *selling* costs—the rest going to sales promotion and personal sales.[11]) It is, of course, difficult to determine which part (if any) of the behavior change (if any) belongs to advertising, and which to all of these other factors controlled by the advertiser attempting to reach the same end.

Then there are those factors the advertiser *cannot* control. The weather, for example, and the competition. The state of the economy, the regulatory/antiregulatory mood in Washington or in the state capitols, breakthroughs in technology. And on and on. They too influence the outcome, and are the "givens" that firms may attempt to alter but must inevitably accommodate. With the notable exception of direct response advertising and a few other forms with an extremely tight advertising-action loop, advertising's workings with and against these forces are better determined by an act of faith than by marketing science.

b. *It is difficult to determine advertising's actual effects because of the quixotic nature of human thought and behavior.* It is entirely possible, of course, to have behavior (sales) without advertising. Without scratching the surface, Schudson mentions marijuana and cocaine, scholarly books, racehorses, sailboats, historical-romance paperbacks, and even the Volkswagen bug in its early years. On the advertising-without-sales docket, Schudson finds that perennial favorite the Edsel, the Lady Gillette, the still-struggling Pringle's, men's hats, and other products (should we mention the PC Jr?) all played against oft-quoted statistics of the percentage of new product failures ranging from 23 to 80 percent.[12]

Human beings are, to quote one practitioner, "no damned good" when it comes to always behaving according to plan. A copywriter at an enormously sophisticated advertising agency recently mentioned that a two-year multimillion-dollar campaign for a popular soft drink was simply "wrong." Obviously he and his colleagues did not share that perception before the fact.

Advertising's elusive target is the individual, and, as one sage once observed, since most of us are not sure what we're going to do from one moment to the next, the chances of an outside observer predicting our future behavior are, to be charitable, problematic. If we conceive of the forces at work to influence an individual's observed behavior as constituting a "frame of reference," we must realize that the interaction of factors outside ourselves (e.g., the presence or absence of other people, the physical environment, etc.) and those inside (e.g., our moods, past experiences, current knowledge, physiological state, etc.) changes from moment to moment.[13] To return to the earlier example, we may not be interested in the stereo ad at the moment, but tomorrow, or even later in the day . . .

Given this backdrop of uncertainty, then, much can be understood about advertising thought and practice—some of it trivial, some of considerable consequence:

- For example, the longevity of the commission system of agency remuneration. Given any adequate measure of performance in the marketplace, advertisers would compensate their agencies on the basis of their proven successes on the advertiser's behalf. Lacking that, they frequently rely on a system that rewards the agency not for how well its products (ads) perform, but for how much of the advertiser's money it spends.
- For example, the "me-too" nature of much advertising content. If it is assumed that comparison advertising is "working," we will see a rash

of like advertisements. If the "European school" is held to be moving the masses, the imitators will grow. If yuppies making the right "career moves" are rumored to sell beer, then we will witness many such encounters. Or animation. Or humor. Or computer graphics. Or nostalgia. Or candor. Or . . .

- For example, the lack of true "professionalism" in the business. Here the wife of the vice president scuttles an advertising campaign because she doesn't like the "look" of the female model. There an account executive is browbeaten by an advertising manager about the failure of the agency to come up with some "new, creative ideas." Or witness the pomp and circumstance of the Clio awards midst black ties at Lincoln Center with giant screens for the embellishment of thirty-second color commercials, now transformed from uncertain exercises in persuasive communication to art forms.

Servility and pageantry frequently replace performance, as many accept proxies for the "real" effect of advertising. We understand advertising only if we understand its uncertainty.

4. BECAUSE OF ITS CULTURAL BOUNDNESS, ITS COMPLEXITY OF FORMS AND FUNCTIONS, AND THE DIFFICULTY IN ASCERTAINING ITS OUTCOME, ADVERTISING IS HIGHLY PRONE TO DISPARATE INTERPRETATIONS. We earlier noted that advertising comes with a great deal of baggage, some of which we bring to it ourselves. Ongoing psychological activity tends toward patterning of experience. Sometimes the pattern is in the subject itself—e.g., a picture of a cube—and requires little additional structuring from our own experiences. But when the external phenomenon is fluid, ambiguous, lacking in clear definition—e.g., an inkblot—*we* must supply the patterning. This is, of course, the basis for a great deal of psychological testing.

It can be contended, then, that advertising in contemporary society is highly susceptible to differing interpretations because of its complexity, fluidity, lack of clear outcome, etc. To follow this reasoning, *much of what is seen in advertising depends on who's looking and where.*

To note the obvious, critics "see" advertising very differently than do supporters. For them, the reality is very clearly patterned as exploitation of a frequently hapless (and possibly helpless) public in forms that intrude, debase the language and our symbolic life, and appeal to our worst rather than our best characteristics. Supporters, observing the *same* spectrum, "see" the self-interests of sellers meshing with the self-interests of savvy buyers to their mutual satisfaction through advertising messages that faithfully mirror the totality (rational *and* emotional) of the human condition. These strikingly different perceptions can be explained in part by the past experiences, values, and current aspirations of the observers. Advertising lends itself to that.

There is also the very real possibility that discussants may simply be observing *different* parts of the whole. Business-to-business advertising, for example, is quite different in purpose, content, and media form from most "consumer" advertising directed to individuals. Even *within* a type (say, retail advertising) one can come to quite different conclusions about advertising as an information tool when examining classified vs. "image" offerings. Again, the necessity of beginning any discussion with a definition of the landscape (e.g., "Are we talking about television advertising? If so, what kind?") is underscored.

SUMMARY

"Advertisements" are bits and pieces of reality. "Advertising" is an abstraction from these elements, and much more. At the outset of our approach to advertising in contemporary society we suggest four premises to "clear away some of the deadwood" that the subject attracts. They are:

1. *Advertising must be considered in light of cultural expectations.* Advertising can play different roles in different societies, depending on the set of assumptions held about such fundamental matters as the relationship between individual and societal interests.
2. *The advertising process has varied intents and effects.* There are many different types of advertisers using advertising for a variety of different purposes, arguing against the common tendency to generalize to the "All advertising . . ." level.
3. *Advertising's actual effects are usually not clearly known.* Most advertisers are interested in affecting behavior—usually sales. But because advertising is affected by societal forces, and is only one factor in the firm's marketing options, and because individuals' reactions to advertisements are inherently complex and unpredictable, simple cause-and effect conclusions are elusive.
4. *Because of its cultural boundness, its complexity of forms and functions, and the difficulty in ascertaining its outcome, advertising is highly prone to disparate interpretations.* Advertising can be loosely compared to the inkblot, with patterning through perceptions affected by who is doing the observing and where in its complex overall structure one chooses to look.

These are, we feel, necessary reference points as we begin to probe this fascinating subject that Daniel Boorstin has called "the characteristic rhetoric of democracy."[14]

Notes

1. Howard Gossage, "How to Want to Do Better Advertising," *Penn State Journalist,* January, 1963, p. 1.

2. Walton Hamilton, "Institution," *The Encyclopedia of the Social Sciences*, vol. 8 (New York: Macmillan, 1932), p. 88.

3. Stephen Fox, *The Mirror Makers* (New York: William Morrow and Co., 1984), p. 381.

4. Michael Schudson, *Advertising, The Uneasy Persuasion* (New York: Basic Books, 1984), p. 13.

5. Hamilton, op. cit., p. 85.

6. James W. Carey, "Advertising: An Institutional Approach," in *The Role of Advertising*, ed. C. H. Sandage and V. Fryburger (Homewood, Ill.: Richard D. Irwin, Inc., 1960), p. 4.

7. C. H. Sandage, Vernon Fryburger, and Kim Rotzoll, *Advertising Theory and Practice* (Homewood, Ill.: Richard D. Irwin, Inc., 1983), ch. 3.

8. Gossage, op. cit., p. 1.

9. Fox, op. cit., p. 380.

10. Michael G. Arlen, *Thirty Seconds* (New York: Penguin Books, 1980).

11. Schudson, op. cit., pp. 20-21.

12. Ibid., pp. 32-43.

13. Sandage, Fryburger, and Rotzoll, op. cit., ch. 8.

14. Daniel G. Boorstin, "Advertising and American Civilization," in *Advertising and Society*, ed. Yale Brozen (New York: New York University Press, 1974), pp. 11-12.

Chapter 2

Perspective: Advertising and the Classical Liberal World View

In the first chapter we observed that advertising can be better understood by examining it in light of cultural expectations. It would seem appropriate, then, to begin with an attempt to explore *the relationship between ideas and institutions*. For, as Carey contends:

> An understanding of advertising rests on an understanding of the nature of ideas and institutions in which advertising found a fertile seedbed to grow. Consequently, much of the modern controversy surrounding advertising is meaningless unless the listener is aware of the implicit assumptions carried by the protagonists about the nature of man, of society, of the economic and political order.[1]

Institutions, Norris observes, "are the 'rules' according to which social life is carried on." They can be thought of as "those patterns of behavior upon which the society depends for the orderly handling of problems deemed important to physical and cultural survival."[2]

And, as IDEAS ⟶ INSTITUTIONS, we need first to understand something about the "implicit assumptions" (or "world views") shared in some fundamental way by members of a society that give form to our institutions. This is, we contend, essential to an understanding of advertising in contemporary society.

THREE POWERFUL "WORLD VIEWS"

Any attempt to classify the incredible diversity of human societies risks ridicule. Yet a great deal can, we feel, be illuminated by asserting that at least three powerful "world views" have characterized many of our socie-

13

ties, and, consequently, shaped the institutions that arise to deal with ongoing societal problems. These are (1) Tradition, (2) Authority, and (3) Classical Liberalism. Some, as we shall see, are far more likely than others to produce what Carey calls a "fertile seedbed" for advertising.

Tradition

Briefly, a society embracing ideas of tradition places a heavy investment in the status quo, often for religious reasons. Things are as they are for a reason, perhaps known only to God. It is frequently assumed that individuals are performing roles in a drama staged by a strong-willed deity or, at least, by stern ancestors. Thus, economic tasks are handed down from father to son, mother to daughter, with "life chances" virtually set at birth. Any deviation would be considered an affront to those keepers of the tradition, both seen and unseen.

An especially compelling example is found in the musical *Fiddler on the Roof*. From the opening song ("You ask me why we do these things, and I'll tell you . . . I don't know. It's tradition!") and throughout the play, Tevye, the milkman, confronts the pain of shattering of tradition as his daughters break from the institution of the matchmaker and his village and its population are uprooted, along with the heavy investment in the past they embody. A contemporary example is found with actor Harrison Ford's detective character's intervention in the culture of the Amish and the ensuing clash of values and actions ("It's not our way!") in the film *Witness*. On a somewhat grander scale, virtually every facet of life in the Middle Ages can be illuminated by understanding the implicit assumptions of the traditional world view, with the ensuing dominance of the medieval church.

Would we expect advertising to arise as an institution under this idea system as broadly defined? It would seem unlikely. Certainly a compelling case can be made that one of advertising's primal messages is a call for change. Change your hair, your toothpaste, your life-style. Aspire to be more. Indulge yourself. Be "all that you can be." These and other siren calls are familiar to us, but would seem both alien and threatening when perceived from a world view of tradition.

Authority

If the world view of tradition relies on direction from the past, authority offers it from the top. Some, it is assumed, are better able to direct than others. They may be presumed to have special connections to God, be proven in combat, hold particular expertise, have been blessed with a high level of intelligence, or possess that elusive element, wisdom. Whatever the rationale for authority, it is assumed that some will direct while others will follow.

Throughout history more civilizations have shared this idea system than any other, with variations ranging from the iron rule of the dictator to the presumed enlightened and compassionate leadership of a popular revolutionary leader. Here we find the seedbeds for institutions as varied as planning boards, concentration camps, five-year plans, and "cultural revolutions."

And what of advertising's presence? On the surface it would seem that a society limiting individual choice would have no compelling reason to call on such a pervasive form of paid persuasion. Certainly Hitler had little need for advertising as we know it. Yet even in highly structured societies there are apparently reasons to attempt to reinforce individual thinking and action, if not change it, and advertising can play a role. Thus we see some advertising in Russia: to serve to inspire in pursuit of national goals; to attempt to encourage particular consumption patterns (e.g., Buy margarine rather than butter). And as planning and decision making are decentralized, advertising would predictably seem more compatible—e.g., advertising is a greater presence in Yugoslavia and Hungary than in Russia and Poland, and is now a growing presence in the People's Republic of China. In the United States the federal government is frequently listed among the top 25 advertisers, with the tasks ranging from attempts to sell in stiff competition (e.g., Join the armed forces rather than take a traditional job), to the promotion of primary demand for monopoly services—e.g., the Postal Service, Amtrak.

Clearly, the world view of authority can be interpreted to allow for the presence of advertising on behalf of the needs of the authority, whether it is benevolent or narrowly self-interested. It is still, however, not the most fertile of seedbeds.

Classical Liberalism

Classical liberalism, Girvetz informs us, was crucial to the "epic transition of the Western world from an agrarian, handicraft society to the urban mechanized civilization of the present century."[3] It presented both an attack on the feudal order and an assertion of basic concepts about man and society that we still find engraved on public buildings, enshrined in the Constitution and the Declaration of Independence, and falling easily off the tongues of politicians at many points on the political continuum. It is impossible to overstate the importance of this idea system to an understanding of American society. What were these powerful assumptions?

The first of them was EGOISM. Apparently the ideas of Hobbes (psychological egoism) and Bentham (psychological hedonism) found the time (roughly the seventeenth and eighteenth centuries) a fertile one. Basically, the egoistic interpretations of "human nature" held that the individual was, by nature, self-seeking. Thus, *all* of an individual's actions—even compassion—could be interpreted as being motivated by self-interest. It is important to realize that there was *no moral judgment* to be applied to the actions. In this context, Girvetz suggests an interpretation of particular relevance to activities of the economic system:

> Passion is no less noble than compassion. And, more significantly in the rough youth of capitalism, the callousness and venality of the most aggressive businessman are morally indistinguishable from the humanity and generosity of the dedicated idealist: each has exercised his preference and, while anyone may err in what best satisfies his preference, here error halts.[4]

In today's age of professed corporate "social responsibility" and individual "humanism" these stark sentiments may seem abrasive—at least in the abstract. Yet, consider how frequently we ascribe the motives of others to naked self-interest—"She's only out for number one." And who would expect to find a text on advertising copywriting without the directive of appeal to the consumer's self-interest woven throughout its chapters?

Individuals, the classical liberals held, were self-interested animals. But there were other dimensions that served to lift us from the jungle.

The most important of these was INTELLECTUALISM. It held that the individual was "rational," to use that much abused word. Unlike the instinct-driven brutes of the animal world, an individual was thought to behave in a deliberate and calculating manner:

> Reason looks to the consequences, carefully balances one promised pleasure or pain against another, and then solely by reference to the quantity of pleasure or pain involved, delivers the verdict. The verdict having been rendered, conduct follows automatically. If the verdict should prove to be wrong, this will be because of imperfect education or inadequate information.[5]

Herein we find the skeletal structure of "economic man," the basic rationale for public education, and, lo, one of the more persistent arguments behind the consumerist's call for more "informative" advertising content, unit pricing, open dating, nutritional labeling, and "counter" advertising. Intellectualism—a powerful idea—embraced, as we shall see, by both supporters and critics of advertising thought and practice.

It is the proposition of QUIETISM that adds a necessary dimension to the idea of a self-seeking, calculating individual. For if, as was assumed, effort is painful, it must follow that a person will expend energy only when there is some definite promise of reward that, on deliberation, seems worth the effort. The implication, then, is that someone pursues various activities—backpacking, cooking, reading—not because the activity is desired for itself, but rather as a means to the end of pleasure. Thus, in the absence of an acceptable stimulus to self-interest, the individual will remain "quiet," apathetic, disinterested. The importance of the assumption of quietism to advertising is perhaps best captured in these oft-quoted lines from Winston Churchill:

> Advertising nourishes the consuming power of men. It creates wants for a better standard of living. It sets up before a man the goal of a better home, better clothing, better food for himself and his family. It spurs individual exertion and greater production. It brings together in fertile union those things which otherwise would never have met.[6]

It is an idea still very much at work in the minds and products of advertising practitioners.

And what of the individual in society? It is appropriate here to refer to *the individual in society* rather than, as contemporary social psychologists would, *society in the individual*. For the classical liberals had drunk deeply of the elixir of natural laws as formulated by Newton and other giants of the time. And if, as the physical sciences suggested, the atom was the fundamental building block of all matter, then must not the person be the essential element in society (ATOMISM)? The whole (society) is thus nothing more than the sum of its parts (sovereign individuals), and the individual is in no way fundamentally different as a member of a society than he or she would be as a hermit. Thus:

> . . . social institutions are created by the fiat of self-contained individuals, they are instruments, even expedients, which the individual can employ or discard without fundamentally altering his own nature.[7]

So the picture completes itself. *The sovereign self-seeking individual is the key.* She or he acts in a calculating manner to satisfy self-interest after it has been aroused by a sufficient promise of reward. He or she creates institutions to further reasoned self-interests and can discard them as they prove unproductive to achieving that end.

Egoism, intellectualism, quietism, atomism—the psychological crucible of the classical liberal "world view."

One emerges with a pattern of ideas which, even though no individual or no generation has embraced it in its entirety, has profoundly influenced the intellectual climate of this country.[8]

How were these assumptions about "human nature" influential in shaping, and supporting, that *economic* solution destined to be compatible with the emergence of advertising as an institution? For it is in the major institution of the market that advertising seems most likely to emerge—and flourish.

THE CLASSICAL LIBERAL MARKET

The market as a system of resource allocation has been so much a part of this country that it is difficult to realize what a revolutionary idea it was.

Ask the typical liberal arts student about the market and he or she will probably offer something about the interplay of supply and demand, but little more. Yet, here was a system that, as classical liberalism itself, "staked it all" on the *individual*. Consider some of the key economic problems faced by any society:

- What will be produced?
- To whom will it be distributed?
- How will it be assured that the work of society will be done?

Under an economic system governed by "tradition," economic roles established by custom are perpetuated from generation to generation. The goods of the society that are not provided within the self-sustaining household are usually distributed in accordance with status hierarchies—more for the feudal lord, less for the serfs, and so on.

Under "authority," on the other hand, economic priorities, and the life chances of the workers in the society, can change dramatically, depending on the whim of the authority structure—planning board, dictator, etc. If the space program is considered more important than consumer goods, human and natural resources will be channeled accordingly.

But consider "the market." It holds that the priorities of the society should be determined not by the cake of custom or the directives of the few, but rather by the aggregate of *individual decisions—all* individuals, not simply the elect or select.

The market emerged in part *inductively*, with pressures from the growing activities of the practitioners of commerce in seventeenth- and eighteenth-century Europe and England. The emerging entrepreneurs sought change, and agitated government to permit their profit-seeking activities to be carried on without undue restraint. And, as we have seen, the market as an articulated system also emerged *deductively*, with the supporting ideas of egoism, intellectualism, quietism, and atomism that culminated in the "world view" of classical liberalism.

If the writings of John Locke still influence our governmental system, there can be little doubt that Adam Smith's masterpiece *An Inquiry into the Nature and Causes of the Wealth of Nations* still shapes the ideology of much of our economic system. (There are no value judgments intended here—merely the observation that the rationale for the classical liberal market remains very much a part of the "conventional wisdom" of much of American economic life in spite of often glaring discrepancies between idea and reality.)

Smith, Heilbroner informs us,[9] was living in a time (the eighteenth century) and place (England) when the division of labor was becoming a dominant economic fact. Thus the decline of self-sufficiency was a major current in his work. But how was this supposed to relate to a system of resource allocation with the sovereign individual as its master?

First, Smith assumed that individuals were self-seeking by nature (egoism). Thus, someone buying goods would attempt to acquire those that brought the greatest pleasure at the *lowest* price and, while in the labor market, would strive to perform as *little* work as possible for as *much* money as he or she could secure. The producer, of course, would attempt to sell the *lowest*-quality merchandise at the *highest* possible price. It seemed a sure formula for chaos.

But the self-seeking individual would inevitably collide with others seeking the same end. What then? Violence? Not if it is also assumed that the individual is by nature deliberate and calculating (intellectualism). For the self-seeking individual, stimulated from apathy (quietism) by an appeal to gain (egoism), will quickly realize that the reward for which he or she has exerted effort will not be achieved unless behavior is modified to some minimal degree. Thus, the producer who wishes to sell a poor-quality good at a high price will have to face the realization that deliberate and calculating individuals will not purchase the offerings if more "rational" choices are available. And the individual entering the labor market may shortly be without work if others are willing to toil slightly longer for the same wages.

But all of this hinges on the assumption that economic power will be fragmented among *many* buyers and sellers (atomism). With many suppliers, it is assumed that some will attempt to seek their self-interests by offering a better economic and/or qualitative value than their competitors. With many potential self-seeking laborers, it is certain that some will work longer hours for less money, and so on. If this fragmentation did not exist, it is easy to predict (according to the classical liberal world view) that those with some degree of power would pursue their self-interest by the exploitation of others.

Thus, in order for the market mechanism to perform its task of resource allocation with greatest efficiency, individuals *must* be stimulated to put forth effort in pursuit of self-interest, they *must* be deliberate and calculating in that pursuit, and there *must* be a sufficient number of buyers and sellers so that no one of them or a few can influence the process.

And on whom does the market shower its favors? On the *efficient*. It is the efficient individual who buys the best quality at the lowest price. It is the efficient wage earner who expends appropriate effort for maximum return. And it is the efficient producer who can offer the highest-quality good at the lowest possible price and hence be rewarded with the patronage of the efficient consumer.

With this background, then, let us now return to the pressing economic questions that, until the evolution of the market, had been answered only by tradition or authority.

What Will Be Produced?

What will be produced will, simply, be determined by what sovereign individuals, in their self-interest, wish to buy. Thus, as Heilbroner observes, the market "has no goal orientation, save to existing demand."[10] If there is a considerable demand for shoes, the fact that shoe supply lags behind existing demand means that shoe prices will rise, along with the profits of the current producers. But the abnormally high profits will soon attract producers from other fields (say, hats) who have fallen on hard times with potential supply exceeding existing demand, thus leading to subnormal return. As hat producers become shoe producers, shoe supply increases until demand is met. Thus, in the long run, aggregate demand determines the types and qualities of what is to be produced. (To use a contemporary example, a demand for pornographic films has led to a dramatic allocation of human and material resources to exploit that demand. It was not decreed by authority that this should be so, nor was it determined by custom—at least in this country—but rather by a sufficient number of individuals willing to part with a certain portion of their earnings for the opportunity to view these epics. As demand slackens, many of the current entrants will seek other lines of endeavor.)

To Whom Will It Be Distributed?

The output of the market system will be distributed to whoever has money to pay for its offerings. There is no welfare built into the pure ideology or its mechanism. As Smith put it, "It is not from the benevolence of the butcher, the brewer, or the baker that we expect our dinner, but from their regard to their self-interest."[11] Social Darwinism is a reasonable approximation of the humanitarian dimension of the market. Those having "marketable" skills who are willing to sell their services in the labor market will be compensated. They may then, in turn, partake of the output of the production sector that is theoretically responding to their demands and those of other sovereign individuals like them. Yet, if the lure of gain is not sufficient to overcome their quietistic nature, the market will offer no rewards.

How Will It Be Assured That the Work of Society Will Be Done?

Again, with the assumption of a geographically mobile labor force (a crucial condition), self-interested individuals will seek employment wherever wages are highest. As we have already seen, it is in production areas of high demand and short supply (to use our earlier example—shoes) where wages are likely to rise. Thus, workers are attracted to those areas of production that are currently high on the economy's list of priorities. Always assuming the lure of gain and the deliberate and calculating path to self-interest, it is assured that, at least in the long run, those tasks that society deems important will be undertaken.

Now, it is important to keep in mind that the market was seen as a system harmonious with the "*natural laws*" of society as articulated by the classical liberals. If supply should fall short of demand, the "laws" of the market would naturally be set into motion to correct the deficiency. Being in tune with "natural" order, it was, of course, self-correcting. It follows that the market, as a self-contained, self-repairing, complex mechanism, must be left alone (laissez-faire) to follow its natural course. Its greatest enemy, then, was, predictably, *any* concentration of power that could disrupt the natural processes of the system. (It is often assumed that government was considered the greatest potential villain in the saga. Not so. Equally calamitous effects were expected to result from concentration of undue—i.e., "unnatural"—power by producers or workers or consumers.)

The self-corrective powers of the market could thus be impaired by any deviation from its fundamental assumptions. For example, the development of a producer monopoly (affecting atomism) would enable the supplier to withhold output, leading to higher prices, etc. Thus, wages and prices would be distorted, and the deliberating and calculating consumer would be thwarted.

"The great flaw in the market," one may hear from some sectors, "is that it provides no incentive for social responsibility on the part of the participants." Precisely. In terms of the pure atomistic market, it was assumed that the participants would follow only one overriding law—do what is best for their own monetary interests. The atomistic force of competition (producers, laborers, consumers) would take care of the rest. For, in the process of "naturally" seeking his or her own self-interest, the individual contributes to the good of the whole (society) "as if by an invisible hand."[12] Indeed, always assuming that the other factors are operative, *the individual who did not seek monetarily selfish ends would be doing a disservice to himself or herself, and to society.*

A clear contemporary statement of this philosophy is found in a speech by Owen B. Butler, chief executive officer of Procter & Gamble:

> Historically, then, our ability to organize corporations for a profit is not a natural right but is a privilege extended by the societies in which we live. The privilege was granted so that we could organize human and financial resources in sufficient mass to take economic risk with the objective of better serving the economic needs of our society through the production of better goods and services at lower prices. The reward, if we succeed in truly serving our society's economic needs, is corporate prosperity which can be used to fund further growth and/or can be distributed to the owners, thus encouraging them to invest in similar ventures. The penalty for failure is that the corporation dies.[13]

There is yet another point deserving of emphasis. The ghost of Adam Smith is far more likely to be called forth at a meeting of the Association of National Advertisers than of the Consumer Federation of America. Yet, Smith must certainly be considered a "consumerist" who regarded the end of all production as consumption and held no lofty illusions about the motives of businessmen:

> People of the same trade seldom meet together, even for merriment and diversion, but the conversation ends in a conspiracy against the public, or in some contrivance to raise prices.[14]

To counter this, Smith looked to the fragmentation of power through competition.

So the sovereign individual—particularly the industrious and efficient—would be the beneficiary in the market. As production increased, so would division of labor and the varieties of goods and services offered in response to aggregate demand. All who would participate would benefit. The lure of gain, the directive of reason, and the discipline of competition . . .

> The market thus determines how society shall invest its resources, human and material. It decrees when, where, and how men shall labor. It determines the disposition of capital. The market becomes the regulator of what shall be produced, its quality, quantity, and price. The market is truly called sovereign.[15]

A remarkable vision.

A "FERTILE SEEDBED" FOR ADVERTISING

After examining the relationship between ideas (world views) and institutions, it seems clear that the perspective of tradition provides the least compatible idea environment for advertising. The world views based on assumptions of authority provide some promise, dependent upon the degree of individual decision making allowed. But it is in the ideas of classical liberalism that we find the most promising basis for the emergence and proliferation of advertising as "world taken for granted."

Advertising as a Classical Liberal Institution

From "egoism" comes the assumption that advertisers can feel free to seek their self-interests through various forms of business activities, including advertising. So also, it is assumed, are potential buyers seeking *their* self-interests, assuming they are aroused from their natural "quietistic" state by appeal to their self-interests, perhaps through advertising messages. Advertisers can, of course, attempt to persuade as robustly as they wish, safe in the assumption that the "deliberate and calculating" individual will not be manipulated. Potential buyers can, of course, sort through the wealth of competing messages (caused by the "atomism" of the competitive structure) and arrive at a reasoned choice. And, who, presumably, is in charge of this directionless, self-correcting system? With this set of assumptions at least, it is the *individual*, who can accept, reject, or ignore, thus directing the flow of societal resources through the full meaning of *consumer sovereignty*.

The seeds of conflict should also be apparent. "This may be well and good," a critic might observe, "but what if people *aren't* active information seekers in their self-interests, or smart when confronted with decision making? What if their choices are, in reality, limited rather than limitless, because of the presence of exceedingly large corporations rather than atomistic competitors? What if all of this self-seeking does *not* work out for the good of the whole, much less that of the manipulated individuals?"

In the next chapter we will address these and other concerns and qualifications about whether or not the classical liberal vision (and advertising's fidelity to it) is still apt. What is important to realize here, however, is the power these ideas have to explain so much of the rationale for contemporary advertising thought and practice.

By way of one example among many, consider a recent advertisement from the American Association of Advertising Agencies (Figure 2-1). It is one of a series of ads meant to upgrade the "image" of advertising, an effort given extremely high priority by the trade association. Examine the "lies" and the assumptions behind the ad's rebuttals:

- "Advertising makes you buy things you don't want." No one, short of actual force, can do that. You're too smart and there are too many other choices open to you.
- "Advertising makes things cost more." Competition, spurred by advertising, promotes the efficiencies of mass production as advertising introduces individuals to products suited to their self-interests.
- "Advertising helps bad products sell." Once you've tried a product, you decide, in some self-interested manner, whether it is of value to you. If not, future advertising efforts are wasted on you.
- "Advertising is a waste of money." Advertising is a friend of the market because it provides information and fosters competition. We *all* benefit.

And the slogan itself—"Advertising. Another word for freedom of choice"—encompasses strong classical liberal themes.

(There are some interesting asides. Note, for example, that it is asserted that it is a lie that advertising *makes* you buy things you don't want. Yet advertising is given credit for "creating" a mass market for calculators. If it needed to be created, was it wanted in the first place? Etc.) The tone of the entire message, however, is clearly set on a classical liberal foundation. Think, then, about this relationship:

CLASSICAL LIBERALISM $\longrightarrow$ ADVERTISING.

FIGURE 2-1

THIS AD IS FULL OF LIES.

LIE #1: ADVERTISING MAKES YOU BUY THINGS YOU DON'T WANT.

Advertising is often accused of inducing people to buy things against their will.

But when was the last time you returned home from the local shopping mall with a bag full of things you had absolutely no use for? The truth is, nothing short of a pointed gun can get *anybody* to spend money on something he or she doesn't want.

No matter how effective an ad is, you and millions of other American consumers make your own decisions. If you don't believe it, ask someone who knows firsthand about the limits of advertising. Like your local Edsel dealer.

LIE #2: ADVERTISING MAKES THINGS COST MORE. Since advertising

costs money, it's natural to assume it costs *you* money. But the truth is that advertising often brings prices down.

Consider the electronic calculator, for example. In the late 1960s, advertising created a mass market for calculators. That meant more of them needed to be produced, which brought the price of producing each calculator down. Competition spurred by advertising brought the price down still further.

As a result, the same product that used to cost hundreds of dollars now costs as little as five dollars.

LIE #3: ADVERTISING HELPS BAD PRODUCTS SELL.

Some people worry that good advertising sometimes covers up for bad products.

But nothing can make you like a bad product. So, while advertising can help convince you to try something once, it can't make you buy it twice. If you don't like what you've bought, you won't buy it again. And if enough people feel the same way, the product dies on the shelf.

In other words, the only thing advertising can do for a bad product is help you find out it's a bad product. And you take it from there.

LIE #4: ADVERTISING IS A WASTE OF MONEY. Some people wonder why

we don't just put all the money spent on advertising directly into our national economy.

The answer is, we already do.

Advertising helps products sell, which holds down prices, which helps sales even more. It creates jobs. It informs you about all the products available and helps you compare them. And it stimulates the competition that produces new and better products at reasonable prices.

If all that doesn't convince you that advertising is important to our economy, you might as well stop reading.

Because on top of everything else, advertising has paid for a large part of the magazine you're now holding.

And that's the truth.

ADVERTISING.
ANOTHER WORD FOR FREEDOM OF CHOICE.
American Association of Advertising Agencies

Reprinted with permission of the American Association of Advertising Agencies.

It does, we believe, represent a strong analytical tool for understanding.

In the next chapter we continue to explore this IDEAS ———➤ INSTI-TUTIONS relationship by examining how well the classical liberal assumptions have fared in the late twentieth century. For, if our idea system is different, so, logically, will be our expectations of advertising as an institution.

SUMMARY

In examining the relationship between fundamental societal ideas ("world views") and institutions, we search for the "fertile seedbed" of ideas that provides an appropriate growth medium for advertising.

It is not to be found in TRADITION, the set of assumptions placing heavy emphasis on the status quo, based on a well-understood societal plan provided by a deity, ancestors, or both.

It may, in part, be in AUTHORITY, with its assumptions of the wisdom of the few directing the many. But much depends upon the degree of individual decision making allowed.

The fit seems tightest with CLASSICAL LIBERALISM, with its assumptions of self-interest (egoism), rationality (intellectualism), apathy (quietism), and the whole being no greater than the sum of the parts (atomism).

Still more understanding is added by examining the *market* as a resource allocation mechanism. Based on classical liberalism, it is assumed to be self-perpetuating and self-correcting, with the good of the whole ensuing from self-centered actions of individuals—"as if by an invisible hand."

Advertising's thought and action can be seen in these ideas. Shopworn and controversial as they may be in the late decades of the twentieth century, they still provide much comfort to supporters of advertising in contemporary society, and useful analytic perspectives to those seeking to understand.

Notes

1. James W. Carey, "Advertising: An Institutional Approach," in *The Role of Advertising,* ed. C. H. Sandage and V. Fryburger (Homewood, Ill.: Richard D. Irwin, Inc., 1960), p. 3.
2. Vincent P. Norris, "Toward the Institutional Study of Advertising," in *Occasional Papers in Advertising,* vol. 1, no. 1 (Urbana: University of Illinois, Department of Advertising, January, 1966), pp. 60-61.
3. Harry K. Girvetz, *From Wealth to Welfare* (Stanford: Stanford University Press, 1950), ch. 1. Used by permission.
4. Ibid., p. 10.

5. Ibid., p. 15.
6. Winston Churchill, quoted in S. Watson Dunn and Arnold M. Barban, *Advertising: Its Role in Modern Marketing* (Hillsdale, Ill.: The Dryden Press, 1974), p. 5.
7. Girvetz, op. cit., p. 23.
8. Ibid., p. 27.
9. Robert L. Heilbroner, *The Worldly Philosophers* (New York: Time, Inc., 1961), ch. 2. The authors acknowledge their debt to the ideas expressed throughout Chapters 1-3 in this excellent work.
10. Heilbroner, *The Economic Problem*, 2d ed. (Englewood Cliffs, N.J.: Prentice-Hall, 1970), p. 547.
11. Quoted in Paul A. Samuelson, "Adam Smith," *Newsweek*, March 15, 1976, p. 86.
12. Ibid.
13. Owen B. Butler, "Corporate Responsibility," a speech given to the Food Marketing Institute, January, 1982. Distributed by the Procter and Gamble Company, Cincinnati, Ohio.
14. Quoted in Heilbroner, *The Worldly Philosophers*, p. 65.
15. Girvetz, op. cit., p. 117.

Chapter 3

Perspective: Advertising and the Neo-Liberal World View

Walton Hamilton offers this perceptive observation on the linkage between ideas and institutions:

> In the continuous process of the adaption of usage and arrangement to intellectual environment, an active role is assumed by that body of ideas taken for granted which is called common sense. Because it determines the climate within which all others must live, it is the dominant institution in a society.[1]

In the preceding chapter we explored the relationship between a particular set of ideas—the classical liberal world view—and compatible institutions (e.g., the market system). Of particular interest was the extremely supportive role these assumptions about human nature, the relationship between the individual and society, etc., play in advertising thought and practice.

But if IDEAS $\longrightarrow$ INSTITUTIONS, and the ideas (or "common sense") change, how will this affect the expectations that we have for our institutions?

Our purpose in this chapter is to hold up several of the key assumptions of the classical liberal world view—spawned more than 200 years ago—to the light of some of the prevailing thoughts and practices of America in the last quarter of the twentieth century. We will attempt to determine what has been retained, and what altered, and to draw out conclusions about the effects of our contemporary world view on institutions, particularly advertising.

We will, of course, be operating on a high level of generalization, attempting not to be exhaustive, but insightful; pointing to events, trends, prevailing modes of thought that seem modal. First we examine several critical classical liberal assumptions. Then we narrow the focus to advertising. It is, we feel, an important undertaking. For, as we suggested in the first chapter, it would seem that much about advertising in contemporary society can be understood as a clash of different perceptual realities, caused by individuals operating from differing sets of assumptions about the world around them.

A REEXAMINATION OF CRITICAL CONCEPTS

Egoism

Certainly a case can be made that the classical liberal assumption about the driving force of self-interest is alive and well in contemporary America. Author Tom Wolfe dubbed the 1970s the "Me Decade," and the 1980s appear to be dominated by a kindred spirit. The much-heralded yuppie life-style is strong on pursuits of the ego—through physical fitness, romance, career moves. The military seem to find appeals of travel, free medical care, and specialized training somewhat more compelling than patriotism. And the world of professional sports may represent the zenith in the naked self-interest business. Of course, much of the past, present, and pending legislation dealing with issues such as pollution control, the disposal of toxic wastes, product and worker safety, and the like, suggests that these matters will *not* be dealt with convincingly unless a *check* on self-interest is instituted.

But are there other currents at work as well? Apparently. Although the mid-'80s are conservative times, and business representatives are somewhat more likely to make statements such as "The first responsibility of a firm is to produce a profit for its stockholders" than in the era of The Great Society, most are still likely to also point to other company activities that seem to have no apparent "bottom line" payout—at least in their short run. For example, it is certainly not uncommon for companies to support programs designed to retrain minorities or support various community organizations and undertakings. Some of this is, of course, clearly enlightened self-interest—e.g., if we don't help make the downtown area a more attractive place we'll have difficulty attracting employees. But other corporate and individual ventures seem to be more reasonably labeled as "acts of conspicuous good will"—e.g., providing financial support to a local theater group, joining with contemporary music stars to record *We Are the World* to raise money for the starving thousands in East Africa. There is, of course, always room for differing interpretations. As a Federal Trade Commission activist observed:

> Americans are under no illusion about business practices. . . . One does
> not have to be a cynic to conclude that those areas where business is per-
> ceived as socially progressive have a striking tendency to coincide with its
> economic self-interest, while those areas where business is given low
> marks for moral and civic virtue happen to be those areas where there is
> little or no (apparent) advantage to be gained.[2]

We can imagine, then, a continuum, polarized by acts of pure self-
interest in its narrowest sense and acts of pure altruism at their most
selfless. Realistically, although there is still a clustering at the egoism
end, that stark position is no longer easily defensible, in public life at
least. Today we *expect* a certain "pulling of the punch" on the part of
individuals, groups, and organizations. *To the extent that we do, we are
assuming that the automatic adjusting mechanisms of the classical liberal world view (e.g., Adam Smith's "invisible hand") cannot consistently
be relied upon to produce societal good from self-interested acts.* Thus, as
our ideas change, so do our expectations from our institutions.

The implications for advertising are significant.

Intellectualism

With Galileo and Copernicus humankind ceased to be at the center of a
universe attended by the sun and planets. With Darwin we ceased to be
the creature unique in its immunity from the forces of natural selection.
With Freud we learned that we could no longer claim to have our actions
determined solely by the reflective deliberations of the conscious mind.
And now we must confront "artificial intelligence." All in all, it hasn't
been easy sledding for our classical liberal friend the deliberate and calculating individual.

But we are a nation that has, in important ways, "staked it all" on the
individual. Thus many of our institutions reflect that belief, even while
others manifest grave reservations:

ITEM: The American jury system rests on the premise that ordinary
men and women, not the elect or elite, can make reasonable judgments
on matters of justice ranging from the trivial to life or death. But these
same individuals may be required to wear helmets when operating mo-
torcycles, thus casting doubt on their ability to make sound decisions
concerning their *own* well-being.

ITEM: Enough faith is put in the rationality of individuals that we are
encouraged to vote for a person (presumed rational as well) who may
ultimately have to make a decision that could destroy life as we know it
on this planet. Yet there is grave doubt whether we should be allowed to
operate our private cars unless first securely strapped to the seat.

ITEM: High school graduates throughout the land hear speakers congratulate them on their citizenship in a land of freedom and opportunity where all doors are open to inquiring minds. Yet these same students may not have been able to find in their school libraries certain "unfit" books whose removal was the result of the agitation of groups offering their standards as the norm to which others should adhere.

As this minuscule sample may suggest, we are apparently uncertain exactly what to make of the presumed "deliberate and calculating" dimensions of what we now accept as "human nature." Clearly we have based countless of our institutional systems (e.g., governmental, judicial, communication, religious, etc.) firmly on our classical liberal beliefs. Yet "common sense" has caused us to question them.

James Carey, referring to Ernst Cassirer's distinction between *animal rationale* and *animal symbolicum*, observes, "Economic man, buying and selling, and equating cost and utility at the margin, has been replaced by psychological or symbolic man who makes economic decisions on the basis of economic and also noneconomic but equally potent psychological need-want stimuli."[3] This is not to suggest that the modern perception is inferior, only that it is different. Thus individuals are perceived as less predictable, more complex, and, potentially, more vulnerable.

Now, recall that in the absence of any conscious "social responsibility," the two principal forces that would channel the individual's inherent self-interest (egoism) into socially beneficial channels were assumed to be intellectualism and atomism. If today we are apparently uncertain about the individual's inherent rationality, or at least uncertain whether it can be depended on, then we can feel less comfortable with the likelihood that the "invisible hand" will see to it that privately self-interested acts have socially beneficial consequences.

The implications for advertising, as you can envision, are intriguing.

Atomism

The sum and substance of much of sociology, social psychology, and like disciplines is that the individual is, to a considerable degree, molded by society. In contrast with the classical liberal conception of society composed solely of sovereign individuals who exercise control through their individual self-interested actions, today we accept a certain level of powerlessness as society and its institutions impose form upon us through their sets of norms, or expected behaviors. This sense of being controlled by societal forces is simply not a psychological state that classical liberals could understand. For, with the assumption of atomism, individuals, not institutions, were the masters.

If societal power is *not* diffused among all participants, then where does it reside? *Still* with "the people," some would contend. But others assert: with big government; big labor; big business; the networks; etc. Clearly seeds of conflict are abundant.

The Justice Department's Antitrust Division was originally established to keep economic competition at least reasonably "atomistic" by preventing mergers ("trusts," etc.) that could presumably nullify competition and pave the way for exploitation. Yet today, William Baxter, head of this division for the Reagan administration, is highly critical of the "populist bigness-is-badness notion." Baxter is apparently willing to assume that companies "got big because they were successful at pleasing customers, not successful at ripping off customers."[4]

By contrast, Ralph Nader:

> The contemporary challenge to giant business . . . is almost primitive in its simplicity. It is a call for corporations to stop stealing, stop deceiving, stop corrupting politicians with money, stop monopolizing, stop poisoning the earth, air and water, stop selling dangerous products, stop exposing workers to cruel hazards, stop tyrannizing people of conscience within the company and start respecting long-range survival needs and rights of present and future generations.[5]

In an attempt to counter what he considers to be a condition of "producer sovereignty" rather than the classical liberal ideal of consumer sovereignty, "Nader conjures up a future in which consumers have their own attorneys sitting across the table from the insurance companies negotiating policies; in which leases are written more in favor of the tenant; in which big buying groups will have more leverage and power to set their own terms in the market place."[6]

Notice the undercurrent of oppressor and oppressed in Nader's arguments. Presumably individuals cannot make their way without joining together—to counter concentrated power with concentrated power, as labor confronts business. This is a far cry from individuals acting in their own self-interests solely as individual entities, not as members of groups.

An interesting parallel is found with the subject of media diversity in our mass communications system. Some contend that diversity in media context can be best achieved by letting the market decide: "Underlying this approach is the premise of a fluid, competitive marketplace and a fairly broad distribution of economic power that will permit all sectors to enter the marketplace and provide needed information-communication services."[7] But another position calls for government to assume an active role to assure a truly "democratic social structure." For, the argument goes, "in this era of giant national and transnational corporate dominance it is absurd to presuppose that there is sufficient equitable distribution of economic power to allow market forces alone to ensure equitable distribution of services. . . . Information should not be considered simply a marketable commodity distributed only to those with the capacity to pay."[8]

Thus atomism, the second major counterforce to egoism, is considered, at least by some, to be uncertain as well. There is no question that much contemporary economic power is concentrated rather than diffused. But a critical question concerns the *effects* of that concentration. Does big overcome small to the benefit of the few? Is there collusion among the titans, and, if so, between whom? Or do we exist in a land of enormous countervailing power blocs, where big business is countered by big labor, held in check by big government and big press, so that a hybrid competition is maintained that ultimately benefits all?

Does advertising, then, flow with these currents or, in fact, help channel them? The answers result in strikingly different perceptions of advertising in contemporary society.

The Economy

Depending, then, on the assumptions one makes about the states of egoism, intellectualism, and atomism, an individual can arrive at very different conclusions about how our economy works and what role (if any) government should play in its maintenance and/or direction.

The market, as seen by the classical liberals, was a self-contained, self-correcting system in harmony with the "natural laws" of human nature and the relationship of the individual to society.

At the time of this writing the American economy is experiencing post-recession combinations of robust growth, low inflation, and declining unemployment, as well as the downside factors of massive debt and trade imbalances. Risk-taking, the entrepreneurial spirit, seems to be much in evidence, with thousands of small firms growing from the evolving electronics and service milieus. *Newsweek* has characterized the movement toward extremely aggressive investing activities as the "Age of Cowboy Capitalism."[9] Much credit for the upside of all of this is given to (and claimed by) the Reagan administration, with its conservative (i.e., free market) economic policies. (It is not without significance that neckties featuring a likeness of Adam Smith have become somewhat of a fashion item in administration circles.)

But for all of this we are still an economy of contradictions, attempting a balancing act of relatively uncontrolled economic activity by individuals and momentous actions by mammoth corporations, labor unions, and government bodies. The Reagan administration, the most conservative of modern times, has been unwilling or unable to make any significant changes in the "Welfare State" programs and mentality that have characterized much of our economic activity since the New Deal. And while actions on the federal level have loosened some regulation strings and placed more fiscal responsibility on the states, the states, hungry for revenue, have stepped up *their* regulatory and revenue-enhancing activities, often at the price of the economic freedom so cherished, at least in word, in Washington. (For example, at the time of this writing, 11 state legislatures are considering 18 proposed bills attempting to raise more tax revenue from advertising services/agencies.[10])

There is still currency given (although not as much as before the 1984 Republican landslide) to the notion of an "industrial policy"—generally considered "a program of government planning, protective trade measures and tax concessions or even subsidies to restore some industrial losers to health."[11] The idea has particular appeal to hard-hit industries such as autos, rubber, steel, and textiles. Failure to compete in world markets, the argument goes, is to a great extent due to government-subsidized foreign competition. Economist Lester Thurow notes the apparent contradictions of firms claiming that business failures here are frequently due to "too much government" while foreign governments are given credit for making *their* firms highly efficient. The core reason for failure, Thurow contends, may not be the role of government, but "bad management, poor foresight and sloppy organization."[12]

"The market," Robert Heilbroner observed, "has no goal orientation other than to existing demand."[13] The ongoing problem of our economy, then, may be seen as when—if at all—to force the direction, to put governmental hands on the economic rudder. There are profound philosophical differences here, ranging from those who see an unfettered economy unleashing the self-seeking energies of individuals and firms for the eventual good of all, to those who see short-run gains turning to long-run tragedies as resources are misallocated to the advantage of the haves and the disenfranchisement of the have-nots.

This "mixed" market interacts with our mixed visions of human nature to provide fertile grounds for controversy. Advertising, predictably, can be seen as friend or enemy of this mixed system, as mirror or shaper of fundamental economic and social tides.

Government

Laissez-faire was a term introduced in France in the eighteenth century and used in the writings of Adam Smith "to argue against the theory of mercantilism and governmental restrictions and regulations of economic activity characteristic of his day."[14] Clearly the idea that government should not interfere with economic activity is no longer endorsed in unadulterated form by even the most conservative among us. Yet there is ample room for divergence on the matter of how much "assistance or control" should be offered, where, and for what ends.

A reasonable approximation of a middle-range position on the role of government in social and economic matters has been provided by economist Irving Kristol. A "neo-conservative," Kristol contended, would generally hold views such as these:

• In general there is approval for those social reforms that, "while providing needed security and comfort to the individual in our dynamic, urbanized society [e.g., social security, unemployment insurance, some kind of national health insurance and family assistance plan], do so with a minimum of bureaucratic intrusion in the individual's affairs."

- There is great respect for the market "to respond efficiently to economic realities while preserving the maximum degree of individual freedom." There is a willingness to interfere with the market for "overriding social purposes," but this, ideally, should be done by "rigging" the market to take advantage of its own dynamics—e.g., housing vouchers for the poor rather than government-built low-income housing.

- There is belief in the traditional American value of equality, but not egalitarianism, "as a proper goal for government to pursue." A favoring of equality of *opportunity* [e.g., Affirmative Action] rather than equality of *outcome* [e.g., "quota" programs].[15]

Now, keep in mind this is a relatively moderate position. Yet it still recognizes and, indeed, encourages a significant role for government.

Government's modern role can be debated as *regulator* and *planner*. The regulating dimension essentially involves government tinkering with what is already present. Often government works in this role to attempt to achieve classical liberal ends—e.g., more competition—even while using decidedly nonclassical liberal means—e.g., government "interference." Clearly the popularity of the Reagan calls to "take government off our backs" and "free the American market system from strangling regulation" suggests widespread doubts about the efficacy of regulation. But we remain ambivalent concerning the proper limits. Columnist Jane Bryant Quinn discussed the Reagan Federal Trade Commission's efforts at "deregulation" in such areas as advertising substantiation, antitrust, deception, and trade rules under the headline "New Handcuffs for the Cops."[16] Apparently, overblown rhetoric to the contrary, we accept the need for "cops," along with our uncertainties about them.

But government also has played the role of planner—to attempt to chart the course of the economy and the society. For example, income tax programs rest on assumptions of future as well as present states—that is, how income should be redistributed in society, what activities are to be encouraged and which discouraged, etc. But there are those who feel that government needs to play a far more active role in order to avert what they consider to be likely ecological or social disorder on a planetary scale. If the world is going to be a reasonably habitable place for our children and their children, the arguments go, government—perhaps world government—must direct resources toward a sane and just future. From this position, the market, and its narrowly self-interested premises, can no longer suffice in a world that may be poisoning itself ecologically and socially. A church publication suggests the limitations of the "invisible hand":

If the entire world were a global village of 100 people:

- 47 would be literate.
- 1 would have a college education.
- 67 would be poor.
- 35 would suffer from hunger and malnutrition.
- 50 would be homeless or living in substandard housing.

Of the 100 people, six would be Americans, with 33% of the village's entire income.[17]

The answer to this dilemma, according to another perspective, is not governmental planning with all its ineptitude and strangling bureaucracy, but a vigorous world market where the benefits will accrue to all through the creation of new economic opportunities.

There is, then, no shortage of arguments supporting government's role as regulator or planner, nationally or on a planetary scale. What is evident is an acceptance of government's role in significant dimensions of the lives of every citizen of this country. This, of course, rests on the assumption that the economy and society cannot be entirely self-regulating without what would seem to be unacceptable social and economic costs—potential exploitation, a widening of the gap between the haves and the have-nots, etc.

This view of the role of government is certainly the most obvious deviation from the classical liberal world view. But our current assumptions about government can only be seen properly against the backdrop of changing perceptions of self-interest, the individual's rationality, and the potential buffering force of competition already examined. Together they represent essential components of our contemporary world view.

We can call this series of compromises and uncertainties "neo-liberalism." They represent, we believe, grafts on the existing classical liberal trunk rather than a new variety. We have, after all, trusted much to the individual, with all that implies, and are reluctant to abandon our ideological roots, no matter how uncertain the resulting idea system.

THE IMPLICATIONS
OF "NEO-LIBERALISM"
FOR ADVERTISING

In the preceding chapter we investigated the implications of the relationship

CLASSICAL LIBERALISM $\longrightarrow$ ADVERTISING.

Here we could begin with

NEO-LIBERALISM $\longrightarrow$ ADVERTISING.

Based on the reexamination of several of the key elements of the classical liberal world view (i.e., egoism, intellectualism, atomism, the economy, and the role of government), we could expect an institution regarded with some suspicion. For if advertisers are presumed to be self-interested, and the presumed counterforces of the individual's rationality and the purifying effect of atomistic competition are qualified, then the potential for exploitation, economic and social, exists. Thus, presumably, the need for regulation—internally (i.e., within the advertising business) based on "social responsibility," and externally, from government bodies.

But there are obviously disagreements about this perception of advertising in contemporary society. Those associated with the advertising business, for example, feel quite differently about the practice and effects of their craft. They are troubled that advertising is viewed as shaper rather than mirror, sovereign rather than servant of the individual. Beginning in 1983, the American Association of Advertising Agencies started an effort to alter the public's perceptions of advertising in America. There was, as chairman John O'Toole noted, no lack of challenge:

> The general public in the United States, in poll after poll, exhibits a misunderstanding of advertising's role, a distrust of advertising, strong negative feelings about television commercials, and a low opinion of the ethics of those responsible.[18]

O'Toole cites these research findings:

- 76% say that advertising makes products more expensive.
- In 1974, 59% of those polled felt that "advertising insults the intelligence of the average consumer," with the 1983 figure at 70%.
- In 1977, 62% of those polled felt that advertising was "mostly honest or fairly honest," while the figure had dropped to 53% in 1980.[19]

One way of interpreting these and other generally unflattering figures is that the institution is somehow out of touch with "common sense," or with critical assumptions of the modern world view. Yet there are certainly contradictions to such an assertion. In the mid-1980s advertising is flourishing. Total expenditures are now being discussed as approaching the $100 billion level. So if this institution is somehow inconsistent with prevailing thought, how do we account for its growing presence?

A somewhat different perspective may be offered by the following:

CLASSICAL LIBERALISM $\longrightarrow$ ADVERTISING.

NEO-LIBERALISM $\longrightarrow$ ADVERTISING.

If an individual operating from basically classical liberal premises "sees" advertising as predominantly a neo-liberal institution, what is the outcome? It is reasonable to expect such an individual to regard advertising as overly regulated from without and overly cautious from within, contending that consumers should be given more credit for their abilities to decide what, if anything, they want from advertising messages, and that, in general, the entire economy and society would be better served if advertisers were allowed to pursue their self-interests (e.g., making a profit) in the most forthright manner possible. Any excesses would be curtailed by the power of consumer choice.

Predictably, then, an individual operating from the more ambiguous premises of neo-liberalism who "sees" advertising as predominantly a classical liberal institution would be concerned about the outcome of powerful self-interested advertisers over potentially vulnerable consumer segments. Regulation would be required.

Following this premise that a great deal of the controversy surrounding advertising in contemporary society can be better understood as differences in assumptions about "human nature," the market, etc., consider the following:

• The Kellogg's cereal company has been advertising All-Bran as high in fiber and linked to dietary habits that have been demonstrated as being beneficial in preventing some types of cancer. Sample headline: "At last, some news about cancer you can live with." The Food and Drug Administration is concerned. If a food promotes itself as having purported medical benefits, should it be regulated as a food or as a drug?[20] *Another* government agency—the Federal Trade Commission—has been *encouraging* advertisers to make responsible health claims with the assumption that the public will benefit. Protectionism vs. self-sufficiency.

• "Corrective" advertising has been a penalty required by the Federal Trade Commission of some advertisers considered guilty of deceptive advertising—e.g., Profile Bread, Listerine, Ocean Spray Cranberry Juice. It requires the advertiser—the original source of the presumed deception—to prepare, pay for, and display, in appropriate media, advertisements meant to undo any advantage gained from the deception. Now, this seems a particularly unflattering view of individual rationality. First, the individual has been deceived. Secondly, it is apparently assumed that she or he will not become aware of the deception unless the *source* of the deception admits guilt. The offending source is required to be the correcting source because, it seems to be assumed, the individual will not make the connection otherwise.

• "Counter" advertising, by contrast, is now back in the news as a result of the current controversy concerning the advertising of alcoholic beverages on television. Based on the Federal Trade Commission "Fairness Doctrine," the reasoning goes that some advertised products—e.g., cigarettes prior to the ban, and now alcoholic beverages—are sufficiently

controversial that broadcasters should be required to allow time for opposing views. The advertising found offensive is not altered, but rather a
"counter" view is added. Note the contrast with corrective advertising.
Here it is assumed that if other messages are added to the "marketplace of
ideas" the individual will attend to them and make a reasonable judgment among alternatives. Different realities from different assumptions.

   • Reflecting on his experiences as a consultant to the Federal Trade
Commission in 1979, Ivan Preston noted the contradictions in assumptions about individual rationality between FTC and business researchers,
and their *internal* contradictions, depending on the self-interests involved:

> FTC witnesses say in effect that the consumer is dumb; so he needs regula-
> tion. Industry witnesses say that the consumer is smart; so he doesn't.
>
> Of course when it comes to required disclosures, everybody jumps up
> and changes sides. The FTC witnesses now assert that the consumer is
> smart enough that he will read the disclosures and act appropriately. The
> industry witnesses now conclude that the consumer is too dumb to read
> any disclosures, or if he does he will get the meaning all confused and will
> think the product is bad in more ways than what the disclosure says.[21]

The reader is invited to provide his or her own examples to illustrate
the often baffling relationships between ideas and institutional expectations.

We have not meant to suggest a mechanistic explanation of the issues
that inevitably surround advertising. Quite the contrary. The human
mind is an incredibly complex instrument whose workings are unpredictable, even to ourselves, from moment to moment. The assumptions we
carry in those minds do, however, affect how we perceive the world
around us. Critics and supporters of advertising can "see" different realities depending, as we emphasized in the first chapter, on who's looking
and where they're looking in advertising's ambiguous field. To attempt to
capture some of those nuances, we offer Figure 3-1, where some of the
analysis of this chapter may be seen as involving personal positions on a
series of continuums composing critical areas in the contemporary world
view.

Note that all the areas are represented by a continuum rather than a
single point of view. This is, we feel, more representative of the complexities of human thought and the interaction of thought with a changing
environment than a unidimensional perspective. Neo-liberalism, as we
hope has been made clear in the previous discussion, is far more ambiguous than its classical liberal parent.

It is, we believe, particularly important to note the scope of "symbolic
man" under neo-liberal thought. Again, there are degrees of rationality
implied. Defenders of advertising, for example, frequently do battle with
critics in this arena, contending that individuals use psychological and
sociological symbolism as pieces of "information" as readily as they pro-

FIGURE 3-1

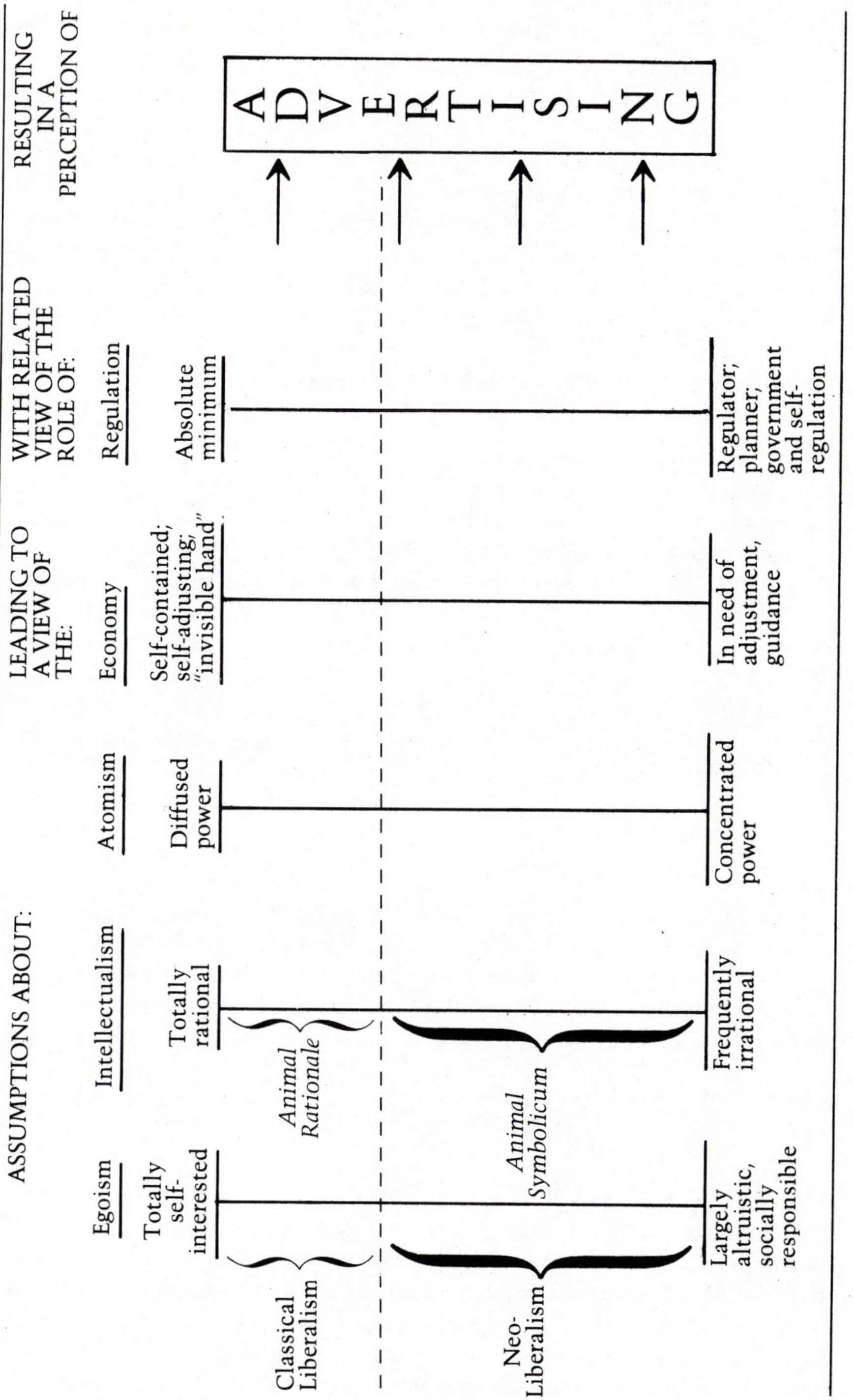
ASSUMPTIONS ABOUT:
LEADING TO A VIEW OF THE:
WITH RELATED VIEW OF THE ROLE OF:
RESULTING IN A PERCEPTION OF
Egoism
Intellectualism
Atomism
Economy
Regulation
Totally self-interested
Totally rational
Diffused power
Self-contained; self-adjusting; "invisible hand"
Absolute minimum
Classical Liberalism
Animal Rationale
Neo-Liberalism
Animal Symbolicum
Largely altruistic, socially responsible
Frequently irrational
Concentrated power
In need of adjustment, guidance
Regulator; planner; government and self-regulation
ADVERTISING

cess such traditional forms as price, quality, durability, etc. Thus the question whether advertising is "informative" enough frequently turns on different assumptions about what constitutes "rationality." Clearly the differences in interpretation between, say, *Consumer Reports* and a typical advertisement are enormous. The former assumes a relatively narrow definition encompassing predominantly objective criteria, while the latter emphasizes subjective satisfactions. (Taken to its logical conclusion, the "objective" interpretation sets up criteria by which to assess "rational" decision making—e.g., price, performance, durability, etc.—while the "subjective" position posits personal criteria—e.g., personal tastes, self-image, social aspirations, etc.—such that no truly "irrational" decisions are possible.)

Now, some contemporary issues will suggest some of the interpretations possible:

• "Advertising is the most effective form of salesmanship for most consumer products and services," says Leonard Matthews, president of the American Association of Advertising Agencies. "It's the least expensive, most effective way to put our sales story before a potential user. . . . It continues to astonish me, however, that many politicians and social engineers cannot or will not grasp this definition of advertising."[22]

Matthews is apparently making certain assumptions that those who "cannot or will not grasp this definition" are not willing to accept—particularly the assumption that the market is sufficiently competitive to place a high priority on efficiency for the many rather than profit-power for the few.

• Frank Brooks, an advertising executive recently returning from a stint in the AAAA Washington, D.C., office, expressed frustrations similar to those of Matthews:

> What left the greatest impression on me was the difficulty involved in explaining the role of advertising to those not involved in marketing, since the view that advertising is an *arbiter* rather than a *barometer* of social norms is becoming more prevalent. As an industry we have a long way to go in convincing those outside our industry that advertising is one of the cornerstones of a free market system and that covert manipulation is *not* the name of the game. Rather, our goal is the dispensing of information important to all consumers. It is the toughest public relations campaign we'll ever face.[23]

Indeed the campaign will be difficult. For it involves convincing critics that advertising reflects rather than shapes, that it deals with discerning individuals in modes that enable them to make intelligent decisions, and that the advertisers' interests are inevitably linked with those of the potential customer such that important information is offered. (The latter would suggest some necessity to alter advertising as an expression of the narrow self-interest of the advertiser by revealing information helpful to the customer—e.g., sugar content, the "parity" nature of some products—but not necessarily in the best interests of the advertiser.)

• Harvey Fineberg, dean of Harvard University's School of Public Health, recently called for a ban on virtually all cigarette advertisements because they promote "the only legally available product that is harmful when used as intended."[24]

Certainly Dr. Fineberg is assuming that cigarette consumption will seem less attractive in the absence of attempts to persuade using "associations with health, youth, sexual attractiveness, independence and an active, vigorous lifestyle."[25] Symbolic man, then, is vulnerable, and cigarette companies are placing their self-interests above their responsibility to a healthy society. Clearly, the accused advertisers operate from a different set of assumptions.

• There is current concern over a wave of children's television programs featuring toys as the central characters—e.g., He-Man, Care Bears, Strawberry Shortcake, GI Joe, and GoBots. The "crux of the issue," according to *Newsweek*, is that "using the most sophisticated conditioning techniques, the manufacturers of children's programming are churning out animated sales catalogs masquerading as entertainment [directed toward] TV's least powerful and most vulnerable consumers."[26]

Clearly the use of terms such as "conditioning techniques" and "vulnerable" suggests a vision of the child as highly impressionable when exposed to powerful external stimuli. Thus the institution shapes rather than mirrors with, again, an apparent lack of responsibility beyond the profit-and-loss statement. But advertisers argue that if these programs were not providing value to the child they would not be watched, and the market would work its way. Children are already knowledgeable, they contend, particularly about products and services within their experience. Thus, this trend *reflects* child interest, not *determines* it.

• Or consider the view of Ralph Nader on the constitution of a true "consumer economy." Here is an economy "measured in terms of consumer well-being, not in terms of the amount of production. . . . Enormous skill, artifice, and resources are used in getting consumers to buy what sellers want to sell notwithstanding the availability of efficient, safe, economically durable and effective alternatives, including that of not buying at all."[27]

The economy, in the Nader view, is not directed from its base, with individual purchasing decisions, but from the vantage point of producer sovereignty. The institution (the market) is thus subverted, owing in no small part to the manipulation made possible through advertising. Frank Brooks's earlier positioning of advertising as "one of the cornerstones of a free market system,"[28] with its implicit assumptions, suggests the dimension of disagreement from the advertisers' perceptions.

• Economist Robert Heilbroner recently reexamined his 1976 statement that advertising is "the single most value-destroying activity of a business civilization."[29] After an interval of nearly a decade, Heilbroner found no reason to recant.

If values can be destroyed by an institution, then atomism is clearly out of whack, and the individual has become servant rather than master. The advertiser response should, we hope, be predictable: advertising can do no more or less than the sovereign individuals allow. It reflects the values of a society (a "barometer" rather than an "arbiter," to quote Brooks) and can do no more.

"Because of its cultural boundness, its complexity of forms and functions, and the difficulty in ascertaining its outcome, advertising is highly prone to disparate interpretations." Returning to this premise from the first chapter, we hope that the reader is now in a somewhat better position to understand the dimensions of the perceptions of advertising— who's looking and where—and their consequences for advertising thought and practice.

SUMMARY

If IDEAS $\longrightarrow$ INSTITUTIONS, then it is appropriate to inquire into what passes for our contemporary "world view" by examining how it may differ from its classical liberal predecessor discussed in Chapter 2.

The notion of *egoism* is now qualified to some extent by the philosophy of "social responsibility," with its inherent assumption that the workings of the "invisible hand" are no longer certain. *Intellectualism* has been called into some doubt because of ambiguity about the dimensions of *animal symbolicum*, and *atomism*, the other major counterforce to narrow self-interest, is confronted with an economic and social landscape dominated by enormous power blocs in addition to somewhat atomistic participants.

Thus the *economy* is now commonly regarded as in need of regulation and, perhaps, direction, often through the role of *government* as regulator and/or planner.

Given this range of ideas, advertising in contemporary society can be regarded quite differently. As master . . . or servant. As friend of the market . . . or foe. As information dispenser . . . or symbol manipulator.

Much can be better understood through such a perspective.

Notes

1. Walton Hamilton, "Institution," *The Encyclopedia of the Social Sciences*, vol. 8 (New York: Macmillan, 1932), p. 85.
2. Michael Perschuk, "The Press and Business: 'As Biased as a Scream

From the Dentist's Chair!,'" remarks before the Society of Professional Journalists, San Francisco, November 10, 1983.

3. James W. Carey, "Advertising: An Institutional Approach," in *The Role of Advertising*, ed. C. H. Sandage and V. Fryburger (Homewood, Ill.: Richard D. Irwin, Inc., 1960), p. 16.

4. "Rewriting Antitrust Rules," *Newsweek*, August 29, 1983, p. 50.

5. Ralph Nader, "Corporate Power in America," *The Nation*, March 29, 1980, p. 367.

6. Jonathan Rowe, "Ralph Nader Reconsidered," *The Washington Monthly*, March, 1985, p. 12.

7. "What Kind of Media Diversity?," *Communication Research Trends*, vol. 4, no. 1 (1983), p. 7.

8. Ibid.

9. "The Age of Cowboy Capitalism," *Newsweek*, May 13, 1985, pp. 52-54.

10. "State and Local Taxes," *The 4A's Washington Newsletter* (Washington, D.C.: American Association of Advertising Agencies, April, 1985), p. 4.

11. "Talking Up an Industrial Policy," *Newsweek*, April 4, 1983, p. 66. Also see "Issues at a Glance," *Best of Business*, vol. 6, no. 1 (Spring, 1984), p. 55.

12. Lester C. Thurow, "Down Without a Fight," *Newsweek*, April 4, 1983, p. 67.

13. Robert L. Heilbroner, *The Worldly Philosophers* (New York: Time, Inc., 1961), pp. 336 ff.

14. George A. and Achilles G. Theodorson, *Modern Dictionary of Sociology* (New York: Thomas Y. Crowell Co., 1969), p. 224.

15. Irving Kristol, "What Is a 'Neo-Conservative?,'" *Newsweek*, January 19, 1976, p. 17.

16. Jane Bryant Quinn, "New Handcuffs for the Cops," *Newsweek*, September 3, 1984, p. 62.

17. "That All May Have Life," flyer for One Great Hour of Sharing from United Church of Christ, 1985.

18. John O'Toole, "Craft or Con?," *Madison Avenue*, August, 1984, p. 32.

19. Ibid.

20. Michael Matza, "Truth in Ads," *Chicago Tribune*, May 10, 1985, sec. 2.

21. Ivan Preston, "Researchers at the Federal Trade Commission—Peril and Promise," in *Advertising and the Public*, ed. Kim B. Rotzoll (Urbana: University of Illinois, Department of Advertising, 1980), p. 74.

22. Leonard S. Matthews, "Beware of Politicians Prattling Pragmatism," *AAAA Newsletter* (New York: American Association of Advertising Agencies, May, 1985), p. 4.

23. "Departing LEAP Praises Program," *The 4A's Washington Newslet-*

ter (Washington, D.C.: American Association of Advertising Agencies, April, 1985), p. 8.

24. "Harvard Public Health Dean Asks Ban on Cigarette Ads," *News-Gazette* (Champaign-Urbana), April 22, 1985, p. 15.
25. Ibid.
26. "Toying With Kids' TV," *Newsweek*, May 13, 1985, p. 85.
27. Rowe, op. cit., p. 19.
28. "Departing LEAP . . . ," p. 8.
29. Robert L. Heilbroner, "Advertising as Agitprop," *Harper's*, January, 1985, pp. 71-76.

Chapter 4

Perspective: Five Prolific Views of Advertising as an Institution

In the two preceding chapters we have probed the left side of the IDEAS $\longrightarrow$ INSTITUTIONS concept. Here we turn our attention to the right side, as viewed through the lenses of five individuals who have asked fundamental questions: What does advertising do? How? With what consequences? Their deliberations deepen our understanding of advertising in contemporary society.

It has been said that "We don't know who discovered water, but we're pretty sure it wasn't a fish." That's a useful idea to bring to the study of an institution. For it is very difficult to appreciate the larger dimensions of something of which we ourselves are a part. Thus, the true impact of the idea "Island Earth" did not hit us until the astronauts photographed it from afar—colorful, but very, very much alone.

And so it is with analysis of institutions. We often find it extraordinarily difficult to understand the full configurations of an institution of which *we are a part*. Indeed, as Hamilton observes, until the academic community began to grudgingly accept the idea that the behavior of individuals could not be adequately explained solely as resulting from their own free wills or as the behavior of cells in a well-integrated and predictable organism, institutional analysis was simply not considered at all.[1]

As we have noted in the preceding chapters, an institution may be seen as representing a convention, an arrangement, an answer to a problem considered important by the society. It was also held that the different "answers" that various societies adopt to deal with the same fundamental problems (e.g., what to produce) can, in part, be attributed to their differing "world views." Thus, the institution of the market (with its emphasis on resource allocation through the action of many self-seeking individuals) was seen to be most compatible with the "world view" of classical liberalism (with its emphasis on the sovereignty and rationality of each individual).

WHY INSTITUTIONAL ANALYSIS?

Of what worth is an institutional perspective? At a minimum, it can give us some view of the forest even as the trees compel our attention. A marriage certificate, a high school athletic jacket, a jail cell make little sense in and of themselves unless we see them as parts of the larger institutional whole of marriage, organized amateur athletics, and a system that attempts to define crime and punishment.

Similarly, advertisements for motor oil, perfume, a breakfast cereal, a bowling alley, or an abortion clinic lend themselves to only very limited analysis unless we first understand why it is we consider an impersonal information and persuasion process an acceptable means to attempt to alter the thinking and behavior of individuals, what the generally accepted "rules of the road" between advertiser and receiver are, etc. Charles Sandage has put it this way: institutional analysis lets us be architects as well as bricklayers, with our vision filled with the total structure as well as the roles assigned to its component parts.[2]

Institutional analysis may also aid us in understanding the "conventional wisdom" of advertising as an institution. Hamilton notes:

> As it crystalizes into reputable usages an institution creates in its defense vested interest, vested habit, and vested ideas and claims allegiance in its own right.[3]

And thus does every institution create its own apology. The origins of an institution may be very utilitarian—e.g., to tend the sick—but as it flourishes and draws to it individuals whose vested interests lie in its perpetuation and ennoblement, an ideology and apparatus emerge to support it—e.g., the American Medical Association. By way of further example, as the institution of marriage comes under attack it is frequently defended by references to the Scriptures, while organized athletics is charged with no less noble an endeavor than "character building," and so on.

It would thus seem reasonable that this perspective may be useful in helping us to better understand not only the defenses of, but also the attacks on, advertising. For example, some critics proclaim that advertising directed to children is likely to do serious harm to their psyches, or that advertising contributes to a massive waste of human and natural resources, or that advertising is offensive and demeaning to women, the elderly, Hispanics, and others. In a similar mode, it is not uncommon at advertising conventions to hear advertising offered as the consumer's best friend, an indispensable source of relevant market information and, depending on the severity of the critical salvos, the bulwark of the free enterprise system. As we hope we have made clear this far, *all* advertising is—objectively—none of these things, despite the claims of critics and defenders to the contrary.

This tendency to generalize about the activities and purposes of an institution is quite consistent with the human psychological tendency toward patterning of experience. We should then be on our guard, realizing that the perception of an institution that emerges from its more dedicated critics and ardent defenders is far more likely to resemble a painting than a photograph, as "vested interest, vested habit, and vested ideas" have their way.

Institutional analysis may, then, lead us to higher analytical ground while reminding us not to overlook the variations in the terrain below. To see the whole while appreciating the parts is, then, not an unpromising quest.

The following five perspectives afford an opportunity to examine institutionally focused views of advertising. Encompassing four decades, they are rich in analytical tools and insights.

CAREY:
ADVERTISING AS
MARKET
INFORMATION

James W. Carey, a communications scholar, offers this intriguing interpretation of what advertising is: "The information provided in purely competitive markets and in primitive markets is *advertising*. We here define market information as advertising."[4] But there is much more that needs to be said.

Carey devotes his 1960 essay to the search for "the *ideas* and *institutions* which favor the development of an economic system in which advertising becomes a part of the very logic by which commerce is carried on."[5] He finds the "ideas" in the liberalism of the eighteenth and nineteenth centuries and, particularly, in the influence of Newton (indirectly) and Locke and Smith (directly):

> For our purposes the ideas that were of fundamental importance in justifying the new economic order [the market] were the notions that all was mechanistic, that natural law governed the physical and social world, that the world was characterized by fundamental harmony, that man possessed reason and conscience, that men were equal and endowed with certain fundamental rights—life, liberty, and property.[6]

The explanatory institutions are thus seen as the market system and, of particular importance, the institution of property rights.

As seen from these classical liberal premises, then, an individual exercises the rights to "property"—anything with which his or her labor is mixed—in the free marketplace, where he or she encounters other individuals in the same pursuit. Harmony rather than discord results because of the essentially rational and moral nature of the individual, and—crucially—the great safeguard of competition. And it is within this system, Carey argues, that the institutional importance of advertising becomes evident:

> One of the fundamental assumptions underlying theoretical analysis of competitive markets, and the whole concept of economic man, is that all entrants into the economic market shall have perfect knowledge; that is, each should be aware of all prices resulting from supply and demand relationships and should have perfect knowledge of alternative forms of satisfying demand. *Caveat emptor*—let the buyer beware—simply means that every individual, being rational, is assumed to possess the ability to exercise correct judgment by basing his decisions on available market information.[7]

Under *purely competitive* markets, the task of supplying relevant information is carried out by the "market" itself (contemporary approximations can be found in the stock market, the grain market, and so on) based on myriad interpersonal transactions. Thus this market-supplied information concerning supply and demand represented the interactions of many buyers and sellers concerning their property rights and, presumably, led to the "natural" value of the goods offered. It is here, in the supplying of relevant information, Carey states, that advertising's institutional birth can be found. It is not, of course, advertising as we generally know it today (it differs in *content* and *source*) but it does, he feels, place in proper institutional perspective advertising's origins as a supplier of relevant information in a market economy.

Advertising in its *modern* form, Carey holds, developed as markets began to lose their interpersonal nature. As production became more centralized, as branded merchandise developed, and as the number of competitors dwindled, the function of supplying market information shifted from the market itself to the participants (firms) in the market, with "the old interpersonal relationships in the marketplace . . . displaced by relationships mediated by mass communication facilities."[8] Of course, the self-seeking firms were interested in "market information" for persuasive (rather than simply informational) purposes.

Now, *under the assumption that the individual is rational,* it is quite appropriate to attempt to persuade. For it is assumed that the rational person will be able to detect truth in the clashing views of self-interested individuals in the economic marketplace just as he or she can sift truth from falsehood in the political arena. Thus, advertising's basic institutional function of supplying information "to facilitate judgment and free choice on the part of the consumer"[9] remains intact, but the fact that the "information" is now supplied by interested parties (firms) in the process has certain consequences:

> There is no longer any guarantee that the self-righting process operates to yield the "true value" of goods when individual firms possess a measure of control over the market. Because competition no longer provides the check on self-interest that it did under atomistic market organization, control in the market is increasingly being sought in human and corporate conscience—a conscience expressed through the notion of social responsibility.[10]

Modern-day advertising is seen by Carey as still performing the traditional function of disseminating market information "as a logical corollary of a market system," but also acting "as an agency of social control providing norms of behavior appropriate to current economic conditions."[11] Thus, as marketing is conventionally concerned with the development of demand in an abundant society, advertising is called upon not merely to "sell," but also to "create and develop" demand for a host of products and services well beyond any traditional definition of "necessity." He concludes:

> Consequently, the nub of the "advertising problem" really rests on a controversy over *who* shall supply the necessary market information, what *type* of information it shall be, and to what ends it should be directed. The reader may then reflect upon the following two propositions: (1) That the source of advertising or market information is determined by the demands of technology and the location of economic power; and (2) that the specific form and nature of advertising messages is dependent on the particular economic problem which the society recognizes as most pressing and, more importantly, on the view that society takes toward the nature of man and to what it is that motivates "appropriate" market behavior.[12]

For Carey, then, the key is the source and type of the information necessary for the functioning of a market system and, implicitly, the assumptions about "human nature" that lie behind these functions. Advertising's basic institutional function is thus linked to the provision of "market information," however that may be interpreted by the society.

*   *   *   *   *

Now, it would seem that considerable understanding is offered by the concept of advertising as market information. If the information necessary for the functioning of a market system is provided by the participants (sellers), then the content and frequency of that information will be different from that provided by the "market" itself—e.g., the grain market. The comparison can perhaps be made clear in this manner:

INFORMATION SUPPLIED BY:	CONTENT	FREQUENCY	EXAMPLE
Market	Factual—prices, quantities, quality	As needed by buyers and sellers	Winter-wheat quantities, prices, and grades
Participants	Biased—whatever is in the best interest of the seller	As desired by seller	Cosmetics advertising

This is the nub of a great deal of ongoing controversy about the proper role of advertising. The content of modern advertising is directed primarily by the best interest of the self-interested "participant" (seller). Thus, it may or may not include *all* the market information that might be necessary for the model of the rational consumer to make a proper decision. To risk oversimplification, "consumerists" generally argue that the informational content of much advertising is not adequate to achieve that purpose, while many advertisers contend that it is. And here the arguments become quite complex indeed.

The consumerist may, for example, argue either (a) that the informational content of the *existing* market information (e.g., advertisements) needs to be enriched (usually through legislation—e.g., the cigarette warning), or (b) that *additional* sources of market information be made more widely available—e.g., the product ratings of government agencies, the judgments of such sources as *Consumer Reports*, "counter" advertising, and so on.

The latter contention seems to suggest a view of human nature much like that of the classical liberals, with its assumption that an increase in message sources will better enable the truth-seeking individual to make a wise decision. Certainly this is the operating premise behind much of the ideology and practice of our press, judicial, and political systems. The former assertion, however, can be viewed as suggesting that man is *not* a "truth seeker" (or at least is a lazy one), and must be catered to by making present sources of market information (e.g., advertisements) more informative (i.e., less "imperfect") in content.

Advertisers generally argue that the individual is quite capable of making satisfying market decisions on the basis of the existing state of the market information as represented by the advertisements of competing enterprises. The key here is "satisfying." While consumerists often assume that economic/qualitative criteria can be applied that will make some products and services objectively "better buys" than others, advertisers frequently suggest that the *individual* should be the sole judge of what criteria to apply in reaching a purchase decision. Thus, it is reasoned, the individual who *bought* it must have *wanted* it, for whatever reason. And if the advertisement led in any way to that decision, then it *must* have been appropriate "market information," at least for *that* individual.

The matter of the frequency of advertising is, of course, a subject of some contention, particularly in the broadcast media. Carey's perspective enables us to see that the frequency of market information, when supplied by self-interested participants, will be whatever they feel is necessary to achieve their ends. Thus, we find the irritation factor emerging among those who complain of interruptions of broadcast programming, repetition of particular advertisements, and so on. Basically, in the classical liberal market, the "deliberate and calculating" individual seeks out "market"-supplied information. With information provided by self-seeking participants, however, the information frequently seeks out the individual, with all the ensuing trade-offs.

Carey's analysis, then, raises a major question for the analysis of advertising: *What should be the proper source, content, and frequency of market information in the United States?* The position an individual takes, as this brief analysis is meant to suggest, is heavily dependent upon such contentions as how rational the consumer is assumed to be.

NORRIS: THE QUEST FOR MARKET POWER

In his 1965 address to the American Academy of Advertising,[13] Vincent P. Norris, another communications scholar, chastised advertising educators for (a) not pursuing institutional analysis in their examination of advertising, and (b) not being aware of the "conventional wisdom" of the institution of advertising that they themselves often embrace (and pass on to their students) in an unquestioning manner—e.g., "The Sunday *New York Times* would cost the reader $5.00 if it weren't for the support of advertisers." (But, Norris points out, without advertising the *Times* would be far less expensive to print, not to mention the savings in the elimination of the advertising department.)[14]

"Institutions," Norris reminded his listeners, "are the 'rules' according to which social life is carried on, and consequently our understanding of the life of any society is limited by our understanding of those institutions."[15]

To understand advertising as an institution, Norris holds, one must avoid the temptation to trace it back to Pompeii or medieval Europe. Such a practice, he contends, is "roughly analogous to tracing the history of man back to the paramecium."[16] Advertising, for Norris, was only "on its way" to becoming an institution "when some sizable segment of the pop-

ulation (namely, the business class) came to look upon advertising not as
an emergency measure to be used sporadically, but as the routine manner
of solving an omnipresent problem (let us say, the profitable conduct of
business)."[17]

He argues that it was not until the last thirty years of the nineteenth
century in America that advertising emerged as a "full-fledged" institution. It was during this period that advertising volume increased tenfold
but, of far greater importance, the increase was due largely to "an entirely
new form of advertising"—the advertising of *producers*, not retailers. Yet,
Norris claims, when authors of advertising texts deal with the emergence
of "national" (producer) advertising, they usually handle it something
like this:

> As the Industrial Revolution brought technological advances, the output
> of the factory increased. Soon it was turning out goods in quantities far too
> great to be consumed in its immediate area; consequently, the manufac-
> turer began shipping his output to more and more distant markets. And of
> course, *he had to use advertising, because the people in those areas did not
> know of him or his products.*[18]

This explanation, he asserts, is a gross oversimplification ("to say it as
charitably as possible") because: (a) centralized supply had existed for
centuries (e.g., the Phoenicians) without advertising; (b) these nine-
teenth-century producers were essentially operating in a seller's market,
so there was no *incentive* to advertise for reputational reasons; and (c) it
ignores the role of the wholesaler—"somewhat akin to describing the
plot of *Othello* without mentioning Iago."[19]

Briefly, as producers began to satisfy the demand of their local
markets they faced the question of how to distribute their goods to other
cities, towns, and villages. For most suppliers, wholesalers filled the
vacuum by serving as the link between a limited number of producers
and a much larger number of retailers. As goods were still largely undif-
ferentiated (e.g., the "cracker barrel" full of unbranded crackers), the
wholesaler was in a position to translate the retailer's wishes ("I need
thirty pounds of crackers") to his own economic advantage by buying
from the supplier who would offer the lowest possible price. And *since
the producers needed the wholesaler more than he needed any one of
them*, he was able to play one against the other. This worked out well for
the wholesaler. It was, however, quite another story for the producer:

> As a result of this price competition, the revenue of the manufacturers
> during this period of wholesaler domination was driven down very close to
> the cost of production. It was to escape from this predicament, to gain
> bargaining power, that manufacturers toward the end of the 19th century
> resorted to branding their output and advertising it "over the heads of the
> wholesalers to the ultimate buyers, the consuming public." To the extent
> that consumers could be induced to request a particular manufacturer's
> brand from the retailer, the retailer would order it from the wholesaler ("I

need 30 pounds of Fenstermaker's Crackers"], who in turn would be forced to buy it from that manufacturer and no other. Now the manufacturer, not the wholesaler, was dominant, and he could name his price.[20]

Thus, Norris contends, *the reasons for the growth of national advertising had little to do with problems of selling per se,* for the producer could sell all he could produce, as long as he was willing to accept the wholesaler's price. "The sole purpose of national advertising, in its early days, was to avoid competing on a price basis."[21]

Now, this intended function was of great institutional import, because it totally "*changed* the pattern of economic activity."[22] For with national advertising and branding, Norris asserts, competition became much less "perfect," and:

- Resources were no longer distributed only to the most economically efficient market entrants.
- Competition was no longer solely on the basis of price.
- There was a tendency for a firm with some market power to withhold production somewhat, thus leading to a "waste of resources."

Basically, then, for Norris, advertising became a major institution in the latter part of the nineteenth century. Producer ("national") advertising emerged in an attempt to acquire market power and thus avoid damaging price competition. The market, he contends, was never the same again.

*   *   *   *   *

Norris directs our attention to advertising's institutional functioning in terms of its economic consequences. First, he suggests it is fruitful to consider advertising's institutional functioning in terms of a dominant *type* of advertising—in this case, that of producers. This in itself has interesting implications. At the beginning of this chapter we suggested that one facet of "institutional behavior" is a tendency to generalize, to see a uniformity among often diverse and conflicting activities. If we examine only such forms of advertising as retail, industrial, business, professional, classified, and so on, it may well be that a cogent case can be made—even today—for advertising's role as a provider of relatively factual information. Such an argument would, however, seem somewhat dubious when we consider much of the advertising of beer, cosmetics, cigarettes, etc. Thus, Norris suggests that focusing on a somewhat narrow analytic field can lead to greater understanding of the role of advertising.

Norris leaves little doubt that he feels the market system in this country changed with the emergence of national advertising as the ongoing solution to a problem concerning the acquisition of market power by the firms in the market. Interestingly, he has forced us to examine the alteration of one form of market system, in which all entrants are essentially powerless to affect the overall allocation of resources, to a variant in which producers can acquire market power through differentiating their products with national advertising. What are the outcomes in this "imperfect" market resulting from the emergence of producer advertising? Representative views would include the following:

Positive

- Advertising enables the producer to achieve "pure" profits that can in turn be plowed back into product improvement, research and development, etc.
- Advertising, as an expression of property rights, is an efficient form of communicating the advantages of the producer's product to a large number of potentially interested people.

Negative

- Advertising enables a producer to manipulate price to his or her own advantage. The price thus has little relationship to the "real" market value of the product.
- Advertising leads to a waste of resources by shifting the reward system away from the standard of pure efficiency and by enabling producers to operate at less than full capacity for their own advantage.

Norris makes his own position clear. "As advertising works better and better," he asserts in a deliberately ungrammatical but telling phrase, "the market works worse and worse." Note that he is working from the assumptions of the "perfect" market, and is assuming that the alterations presumably caused by advertising are, overall, dysfunctional. Herein, it can be contended, lies the primary analytical rigor in his analysis, as the source and content of market information served for Carey.

For Norris is offering a critical economic perspective that explains much about the assumptions behind many of the more persistent economic criticisms of advertising. For example:

- "Advertising leads to higher prices"—based on *what standard?*
- "Advertising restricts competition"—compared to *what?*
- "Advertising leads to a waste of resources"—defined *how?*

Basically, it can be contended that these familiar claims are all assuming that "as advertising works better and better, the [perfect] market works worse and worse." At a very minimum, then, Norris's perspective forces us to probe the implicit standard behind critical economic themes concerning advertising and the economy, and weigh that model with its contender.

Herein, then, is both a more historically precise explanation of the origins of national advertising, *and* a critical matrix for examining advertising's performance in differing visions of a market system.

POTTER:
SOCIAL CONTROL
WITHOUT SOCIAL
RESPONSIBILITY

It was really an "outsider"—a historian—who first dealt with the idea of advertising as an institution in an explicit analysis. David Potter,[23] in his 1954 book, *People of Plenty*, explored the role of abundance in society. Abundance, he contended, must be considered "a major force" in American history, comparable in importance to democracy, religion, and science. Yet unlike those other forces, abundance has apparently not been viewed as having its own distinctive institution comparable to representative government for democracy, the clergy for religion, and the apparatus of scholarship for science. Potter felt that he had found the appropriate institution of an abundant society:

> If we seek an institution that was brought into being by abundance, without previous existence in any form, and, moreover, an institution which is peculiarly identified with American abundance rather than abundance throughout Western civilization, we will find it, I believe, in modern American advertising.[24]

Advertising, he feels, has been woefully neglected by historians of public opinion, popular culture, and the mass media, even though "advertising created modern American radio and television, transformed the modern newspaper, evoked the modern slick-periodical, and remains the vital essence of them at the present time."[25]

Potter notes the considerable growth of advertising in the last quarter of the nineteenth century, and particularly the rise of the advertising of producers (Norris's emphasis) in an attempt to "create a consumer demand for their brand and thus of exerting pressure upon the distributor to keep their products in stock."[26] Soon, Potter contends, producers were no longer using advertising merely "as a coupling device between existing market demand and their own supply," but rather were trying "to create a demand."[27] This, he feels, altered the nature of the advertising message from one emphasizing information to one focused "upon the desires of the consumer." (He notes the appearance, in 1903, of Walter Dill Scott's article, "The Psychology of Advertising.")

What accounts for advertising's growth? Potter quotes Neil Borden's explanation of the widening gap between producer and consumer, placing particular emphasis on Borden's claim that advertising flourished in part when "the quest for product differentiation became intensified as the industrial system became more mature, and as manufacturers had capacity to produce far beyond existing demand."[28]

Advertising begins to fill its essential function in the society, Potter holds, when potential supply exceeds existing demand—a condition of abundance. And what, beyond the aims of the individual producers, does advertising accomplish in this capacity?

> . . . consumer societies, like all other kinds, seem to fall short of their utopias, and we revert to the question how the citizen, in our mixed production-consumption society, can be educated to perform his role as a consumer, especially as a consumer of goods for which he feels no impulse of need. Clearly he must be educated, and the only institution which we have for instilling new needs, for training people to act as consumers, for altering men's values, and thus for hastening their adjustment to potential abundance is advertising. That is why it seems to me valid to regard advertising as distinctively the institution of abundance.[29]

Thus, Potter contends, advertising's influence is not merely economic. In fact, he asserts it is one of a very few "instruments of social control" that serve to "guide the life of the individual by conceiving of him in a distinctive way and encouraging him to conform as far as possible to the concept."[30] The following summarizes his view of the nature of these "instruments of social control":[31]

INSTITUTION	CONCEIVES OF THE INDIVIDUAL AS:	APPEALS TO:
The church	An immortal soul	Salvation, through conscience, spirit
The schools	A being whose behavior is guided by reason	Reason, with the hope of a perfected society
Industry	A productive agent	Workmanship, personal satisfaction
Advertising	A consumer	Desires and wants—cultivated or natural

Though the church, the schools, and industry "have tried to improve man and to develop in him qualities of social value," Potter feels that advertising has fallen short:

> It is this lack of institutional responsibility, this lack of inherent social purpose to balance social power which, I would argue, is a basic cause for concern about the role of advertising.[32]

Potter devotes the remainder of his chapter to developing what he considers to be the dimensions of advertising's "power." First, there is the sheer dollar weight—e.g., "Our national outlay for the education of citizens . . . amounted to substantially less than our expenditure for the education of consumers."[33] But of particular concern to Potter is advertising's "profound influence on the media" and "through them" on the public.[34]

He asserts that as advertising revenues became more and more attractive to publishers—and essential to broadcasters—their products (magazines, newspapers, television and radio programs) became less and less *ends* in themselves and more *means* to the end of attracting large numbers of potential customers to be exposed to the advertising messages. This necessitated watering down the nonadvertising content of the media—avoiding controversial themes, emphasizing the bland "common denominator" that would attract the largest numbers of readers or viewers, and other similar strategies. Thus, he contends, Americans are more frequently titillated by the mass media than educated, the appeal is to the attention-getting rather than the substantive, and so on. The result of all this is thus "to enforce already existing attitudes, to diminish the range and variety of choices and, in terms of abundance, to exalt the materialistic values of consumption."[35] He summarizes:

> Certainly it marks a profound social change that this new institution for shaping human standards should be directed, not as are the school and the church, to the inclination of beliefs or attitudes that are held to be of social value, but rather to the stimulation or even the exploitation of materialistic drives and emulative anxieties and then to the validation, the sanctioning, and the standardization of these drives as accepted criteria of social value. Such a transformation, brought about by the need to stimulate desire for the goods which an abundant economy has to offer and which a scarcity economy would never have produced, offers strong justification for the view that advertising should be recognized as an important social influence and as our newest major institution—an institution peculiarly identified with one of the most persuasive forces in American life, the force of economic abundance.[36]

For Potter, then, advertising is an institution of abundance whose important effects are not merely economic but rather "upon the values of our society"[37] as an instrument of social control. Clearly, he does not view the outcome positively.

*   *   *   *   *

Potter links advertising's institutional functioning to the transition from a "producer's culture" to a "consumer's culture." Advertising, he contends, teaches us to be consumers. In this capacity, advertising becomes one of a handful of institutions that exert "social control." The problem, as Potter sees it, is that the other major sources of social control—the schools, the church, the business system—have a higher "social responsibility," a noble vision of man to go with their social power. Advertising,

Potter contends, does not, and this lack of higher purpose is a cause of considerable concern to him.

Remember that under the classical liberal world view there was *no* explicit expectation of responsibility beyond individual self-interest. Indeed, the "laws" of the market would operate in their self-correcting manner only if each participant pursued his or her self-interest in a single-minded manner. The forces of competition (and man's inherent moral sense) would—at least in the long run—assure that all would work out well for the whole because of the "universal harmony of interests" or, if you prefer Adam Smith's phrase, the "invisible hand."

To the extent that Potter is chiding advertising for its lack of social responsibility, he is operating from a set of assumptions about "human nature" more closely aligned with neo-liberalism than with its classical liberal predecessor. Thus, Potter, by implication, seems to be arguing that the individual will not be able to resist the seductive appeals of advertising to his or her "wants and desires" *in spite of the competition offered by the other major institutions he offers for comparison.* Under these assumptions it is not surprising that he calls for less self-interest and more "social" interest on the part of advertisers.

It can further be assumed that from this perspective many of the "natural laws" of the classical liberals are no longer considered operative. Primary among the apparent defections are the decline of man's rationality under the onslaught of high advertising expenditures and the assumption that a "clash of ideas" will emerge from the normal functioning of the media system. (In fact, Potter asserts, because the media depend on advertising they serve basically as perpetrators of the status quo in a dollar-sensitive quest to offend no one and thus maximize the audience size they sell to advertisers.)

More explicitly, Potter's view raises intriguing questions in the very broadest realms of "social control." Are massive doses of advertising necessary to sustain a "consumer culture"? And, if they are, what are their costs—in terms of the cliché-like "leading us to buy things we don't need or want," in the watered-down, status-quo–oriented values that the advertising-dependent media must perpetuate in order to survive, and so on? (It is important to note that in today's era of increasing media fragmentation, Potter's assertions of media homogeneity and editorial timidity do not appear as persuasive as they might have in the early 1950s. This should not, however, deter the serious student from careful consideration of Potter's primary contribution to understanding and examination—the idea of advertising's presumed institutional directive to "teach us to be consumers" with all that it implies.)

Now, if Carey offers us analytical perspectives on advertising's communication dimensions, and Norris insights into critical economic themes, Potter helps us to understand the assumptions behind the criticisms of advertising as a *social* force.

Consider issues such as:

- Does advertising adversely influence children?
- Does advertising cause social strains through stereotyping?
- Does advertising "cause us to buy things we don't want or need"?

The answers, for the critics, would be *yes*. Why? Because all critics basically assume, as did Potter, that advertisers' self-interests are *not* channeled toward socially desirable ends by individual rationality and/or the forces of competition. Thus, in the absence of "social responsibility," exploitation reigns.

In essence, Potter offers us insights into the frequent event of a neo-liberal perspective interacting with an institution seen to be operating from classical liberal premises. Small wonder, then, that Potter's perspective has endured, for it illuminates areas of bedrock conflict.

SANDAGE:
TO INFORM
AND PERSUADE

Advertising educator Charles Sandage addressed his 1973 essay[38] to the climate of criticism that surrounded advertising in the 1960s-1970s phase of "consumerism." He makes it clear from the outset that an institutional perspective can enable the practitioner to *respond to criticism* by "understanding the true nature of advertising and concentrating on its positive values."[39]

Thus, he asserts, it is first necessary to distinguish between the institution (advertising) and the instruments (advertisements). Much criticism, and much heated defense, has been spent on individual parts of the larger whole. But what is the nature of the whole?

Advertising, Sandage holds, has been assigned the function of "helping society to achieve abundance" by *informing* and *persuading* members of society with respect to products, services, and ideals.[40] In addition, another responsibility "that is becoming more and more significant is that of education in consumerism—the development of judgment on the part of consumers in their purchase practices."[41] Once we understand these larger functions, we will also realize that a great deal of the criticism of advertising is in fact criticism of such basic concepts as abundance, persuasion, and freedom of choice. The classical liberal tone of his argument is perhaps best revealed in his comments on freedom of choice:

> In a free society the nature of consumption is determined primarily by consumers themselves. They decide, through their actions in the marketplace, how many people will be employed to supply them with tobacco, clothing, homes, automobiles, boats, golf balls, cosmetics, air conditioners, books and paintings to hang on their walls. They decide, too, how much

of their purchasing power will be spent to support preachers, private schools, research foundations, art galleries and symphony orchestras. In a little different fashion but still basic, they determine through their votes at the polls how much they will buy in the form of defense hardware, public school buildings, teachers' services, public parks, highways, help for the less fortunate, and pollution control.[42]

To the extent that individuals do *not* seem to be making choices that, objectively, appear to be in their best interests, the solution rests, he contends, not in "substituting a commissar for the free consumer," but rather in "raising the level of education in consumerism." Thus, Sandage argues, advertising should serve to "implement freedom of choice" by "supplying consumers with adequate and accurate information about all of the alternatives available to them."[43]

He suggests that this necessary flow of information will be accomplished through two processes:

1. Through the ongoing conflict of ideas in the marketplace—e.g., the overweight person is exposed not only to the tempting messages of the confectioners, but also to the persuasive arguments for the products and services of weight reduction.
2. Through "full and honest disclosure, with competition available to provide knowledge of alternatives." This suggests that each message "will provide full disclosure of product characteristics that are important in evaluating its ability to meet a need or want."[44]

By performing these two functions, Sandage asserts, those who attempt to "inform and persuade" in respect to "things, services, and ideas" are indeed involved in socially beneficial activities. For "it is a proper and justifiable social goal to help consumers maximize their satisfactions."[45]

Stepping back to an institutional perspective, Sandage contends, offers the practitioner of advertising the opportunity to assess the function that society expects advertising to perform. That function, he asserts, is to help society achieve abundance by informing and persuading its sovereign citizens in relation to products, services, and ideas. Thus, he reasons, "Advertising practitioners who accept this concept are indeed consumer advocates."[46]

*   *   *   *   *

The sovereign consumer is clearly in charge in Sandage's view of the system. It is the individual's decisions that determine what will be produced, in what quantities, of what quality, and so on. In direct contention with Potter's "social control" interpretation, he asserts:

Advertising is criticized on the ground that it can manipulate consumers to follow the will of the advertiser. The weight of evidence denies this ability. Instead, evidence supports the position that advertising, to be successful, must understand or anticipate basic human needs and wants and interpret available goods and services in terms of their want-satisfying abilities.[47]

The institution is not master here, but servant. This is, in general, quite consistent with the strongly classical liberal perspective of the Sandage analysis.

It should be noted, however, that he also suggests that the quality of the information supplied by advertisers *is not* always sufficient to enable the sovereign individual to function rationally. Thus he calls for "full and honest disclosure" in advertising. Carried to its full interpretation, this could at times require the disclosure of information by advertisers that is not in their best interests—e.g., the advertisers of smaller cars providing the information that loss of life in event of accident is far more likely in their products than in full-size models. This would, of course, represent a not insignificant qualification of the classical liberal directive of the pursuit of self-interest. It does not, however, seriously dilute the strength of the contrast between the different philosophical assumptions held by Sandage and the other major theorist of advertising and abundance, David Potter. Sandage, it is clear, inevitably comes down on the side of the *sovereign individual*—the true litmus test for a person with a strong classical liberal orientation.

If Carey offers insights in advertising's dimensions as market information, Norris economic criticisms, and Potter social critiques, clearly the Sandage perspective illuminates advertising's positive posture:

- Advertising *cannot* "cause us to buy things we don't want or need."
- Advertising interprets the want-satisfying qualities of products and services for the ultimate benefit of the individual.

Why? Because the *individual is capable*—capable of seeking, capable of evaluating, capable of finding satisfaction from the market. Advertising, then, can do no more than the individual finds meaningful.

These sentiments, as we have seen, are easily found in the advertising business. Their basically classical liberal orientation is, again, apparent.

SCHUDSON:
ADVERTISING AS
CAPITALIST REALISM

Perhaps the central conceptual contribution from sociology/communications scholar Michael Schudson's 1984 book, *Advertising, the Uneasy Persuasion*,[48] is the contention that advertising in America (at least the national consumer goods variety) can be seen as "capitalist realism."

Unlike efforts of personal selling, Schudson argues, advertising "is part of the establishment and reflection of a common symbolic culture" which "connects the buyer to an assemblage of buyers through words and pictures available to all of them and tailored to no one of them."[49] He then explores the dimensions and consequences of that culture.

In advertising, he contends, experience is "flattened" in the sense that advertisements depict life that is relatively timeless and placeless. People in advertisements are meant to be regarded not as distinct individuals but rather as representations of a "social type or a demographic category" with which the reader or viewer can identify. These neither real nor totally fictional messages are then seen as linked "to the political economy whose values they celebrate and promote."[50] Hence, "capitalist realism."

Advertising as a form of symbolic value expression can be seen with greater clarity, Schudson states, by comparing it to socialist realism, and the guidelines for socialist realist art:

1.   Art should picture reality in simplified and typified ways so that it communicates effectively to the masses.
2.   Art should picture life, but not as it is so much as life as it should become, life worth emulating.
3.   Art should picture reality not in its individuality but only as it reveals larger social significance.
4.   Art should picture reality as progress toward the future and so represent social struggles positively. It should carry an air of optimism.
5.   Art should focus on contemporary life, creating pleasing images of new social phenomena, revealing and endorsing new features of society and thus aiding the masses in assimilating them.[51]

The parallels, Schudson continues, are striking:

> American advertising, like socialist realist art, simplifies and typifies. It does not claim to picture reality as it is but reality as it should be—life and lives worth emulating. It is always photography or dramas or discourse with a message—rarely picturing individuals, it shows people only as incarnations of larger social categories. It always assumes that there is progress. It is thoroughly optimistic, providing for any troubles that it identifies a solution in a particular product or style of life. It focuses, of course, on the new, and if it shows some signs of respect for tradition, this is only to help in the assimilation of some new commercial creation.[52]

Of course, unlike socialist realism, advertising is not state art, except in the sense that it is accepted as a significant phenomenon in society. Yet, its functions are similarly linked to the supporting culture, as "without a masterplan of purposes [advertising] glorifies the pleasures and freedoms of consumer choice in defense of the virtues of private life and material ambitions."[53] Thus, the satisfactions portrayed in this idealization of the consumer are "invariably private," as individuals are "encouraged to think of themselves and their private worlds" rather than any form of collective values.[54]

Advertising as an art form, Schudson contends while citing Krugman and others, need not necessarily command belief to be effective. Indeed, "it may shape our sense of values even under conditions where it does not greatly corrupt our buying habits."[55] Because we often do not take advertising seriously, our "perceptual defenses" are relatively open.[56]

This openness becomes even more plausible because advertising is essentially confronting us with values with which we already basically agree. Thus advertising's institutional function can be seen as *materializing a way of experiencing a consumer way of life*. "Making the implicit explicit is necessary to engage and renew a whole train of commitments, responsibilities, and possibilities."[57] In the same way that married couples continue to make the "implicit explicit" by stating, "I love you," advertising, Schudson contends, "is capitalism's way of saying 'I love you' to itself."[58]

And what are the consequences of this reaffirmation of widely shared values?

> Advertising does not make people believe in capitalist institutions or even in consumer values, but so long as alternative articulations of values are relatively hard to locate in the culture, capitalist realist art will have some power.[59]

Advertising, of course, has no monopoly in the symbolic marketplace, Schudson adds, but "advertising has a special cultural power" since:

- no other cultural form is as accessible to children
- no other form confronts visitors and immigrants to our society so forcefully
- only professional sports surpass advertising as a source of visual and verbal clichés, aphorisms, and proverbs.[60]

Advertising, Schudson concludes, is not a shaper of our values. Yet the values presented so relentlessly

> are not the only ones people have or aspire to, and the pervasiveness of advertising makes us forget this. Advertising picks up some of the things people hold dear and re-presents them to people as *all* of what they value, assuring them that the sponsor is the patron of common ideals.[61]

*   *   *   *   *

There are some clear parallels between Schudson's perspective and that of at least two of the other theorists discussed here. First, like Norris, Schudson limits his analysis to one form of advertising—national consumer goods—while recognizing the different functions of other types— e.g., retail. Second, with his concentration on advertising's relationship to values, he is akin to Potter. What, then, does his perspective assume, and what analytical tools does it offer?

Interestingly, there seem to be mixed signals in relation to atomism, or the seat of societal power. Schudson makes it clear that the values advertising embodies are widely diffused through the society, thus suggesting the classical liberal interpretation of institutions being shaped by the individuals—i.e., the individual in the society rather than the society in the individual. Yet, he is also troubled that "alternative articulations of values are relatively hard to locate,"[62] thus implying that other sets of values do not receive comparable institutional representation—a clear contradiction to atomism.

It can be argued that at the base of the argument is a vision of the individual that suggests a passiveness in responding to values other than those articulated so relentlessly through advertising's ubiquity. Thus advertising re-presents "some of the things people hold dear . . . as *all* of what they value."[63] If individuals are willing to accept the reinforcement of some values to the neglect of other values they also "have or aspire to," then advertising is powerful indeed, and the power shifts to the institution.

Schudson's perspective, then, suggests several analytical modes. Among the more interesting:

1. Advertising's economic impact is not nearly as important as its potential interaction with the societal value structure.
2. Although it could be considered relatively benign in the sense that its values are generally our values, advertising's long-run effect is troublesome because of its pervasiveness and the limited scope of its value themes.
3. Its influence is particularly magnified in certain population segments—e.g., children, immigrants—and becomes even more powerful because of its assimilation as part of popular culture through comedy routines, movies, books, etc.
4. Advertising's effect may be all the more influential because it is so easily accepted as part of our institutional environment and *not* taken seriously, largely because its forms are often subject to derision, and, perhaps of greatest importance, *because we are so comfortable with its values.*

Advertising as capitalist realism. The individual messages are clearly the stuff of the self-interests of individual advertisers. Yet the aggregate makes an important—a certainly debatable—contribution to our symbolic marketplace.

SUMMARY

In an attempt to deepen our understanding of the nature of institutional analysis in relation to advertising, we've examined the views of five theorists.

James Carey sees advertising performing the historically necessary function of providing market information, with the nature of that information, and its potential effects, clearly affected by its source and by attendant assumptions about human nature.

Vincent Norris sees advertising emerging as an institution in the late nineteenth century with the rise of national (producer) advertising in an attempt to avoid price competition and seize market power from the dominant wholesalers. The market as a system of resource allocation was altered significantly.

David Potter finds advertising the distinctive institution of abundance, training people to act as consumers in an abundant economy, but lacking social reponsibility to counter social control.

Charles Sandage envisions advertising informing and persuading individuals to help them make satisfying decisions in a largely responsive market.

And, finally, Michael Schudson suggests advertising as an expression of capitalist ideals—capitalist realism as compared to socialist realism— with significant influence because of its possibility of overwhelming other competing values with its sheer ubiquity and the comfort of its themes.

Each theory, along with the perspectives offered in the preceding three chapters, provides us with analytic tools for arriving at greater understanding of the various dimensions of advertising in contemporary society. It is to a tighter focus on several of these dimensions that we now turn.

Notes

1. Walton Hamilton, "Institution," *The Encyclopedia of the Social Sciences*, vol. 8 (New York: Macmillan, 1932), p. 89.
2. Charles H. Sandage, "Some Institutional Aspects of Advertising," *Journal of Advertising*, vol. 1, no. 1 (1973), p. 9.
3. Hamilton, op. cit., p. 87.
4. James W. Carey, "Advertising: An Institutional Approach," in *The Role of Advertising*, ed. C. H. Sandage and V. Fryburger (Homewood, Ill.: Richard D. Irwin, Inc., 1960), p. 14, emphasis in original.
5. Ibid., p. 3, emphasis added.
6. Ibid., p. 10.
7. Ibid., p. 13.
8. Ibid., p. 15.
9. Ibid.
10. Ibid.
11. Ibid., p. 16.
12. Ibid., p. 17, emphasis in original.
13. Vincent P. Norris, "Toward the Institutional Study of Advertising," *Occasional Papers in Advertising* (Urbana: University of Illinois,

Department of Advertising, 1966), pp. 59-73. A current treatment of
many of the economic issues can be found in Norris's "The Economic Effects of Advertising," in *Current Issues and Research in
Advertising*, vol. 2, ed. James H. Leigh and Claude R. Martin (Ann
Arbor: Division of Research, Graduate School of Business Administration, University of Michigan, 1984), pp. 39-135.

14. Ibid., p. 72.
15. Ibid., p. 60.
16. Ibid., p. 63.
17. Ibid., p. 65.
18. Ibid., p. 66, emphasis in original.
19. Ibid., p. 66.
20. Ibid., p. 67. Quote beginning "over the heads . . ." from Nicholas
     Kaldor, "The Economics of Advertising," *The Review of Economic
     Studies*, vol. 18(1), no. 45 (1949-1950), pp. 1-27.
21. Norris, op. cit., p. 68.
22. Ibid., emphasis in original.
23. David M. Potter, "The Institution of Abundance: Advertising," in
     The Role of Advertising, ed. C. H. Sandage and V. Fryburger, pp. 18-
     34. Originally Chapter 8 in Potter's *People of Plenty* (Chicago: Uni-
     versity of Chicago Press, 1954). All subsequent citations are from
     the Sandage and Fryburger chapter.
24. Ibid., p. 18.
25. Ibid., p. 19.
26. Ibid., p. 21.
27. Ibid., p. 22.
28. Ibid. No specific citation for Borden reference other than *The Eco-
     nomic Effects of Advertising*, 1942.
29. Ibid., pp. 24-25.
30. Ibid., p. 25.
31. Ibid. Interpretation based on his statements on that page.
32. Ibid., p. 26.
33. Ibid.
34. Ibid., basically pp. 27-32.
35. Ibid., p. 34.
36. Ibid.
37. Ibid., p. 34.
38. Charles H. Sandage, "Some Institutional Aspects of Advertising,"
     Journal of Advertising, vol. 1, no. 1, pp. 6-9. Copyright 1973. Re-
     printed with permission by Board of Directors, *Journal of Adver-
     tising*.
39. Ibid., p. 6.
40. Ibid.
41. Ibid., pp. 6-7.
42. Ibid., p. 7.

43. Ibid.
44. Ibid., p. 8.
45. Ibid.
46. Ibid.
47. Ibid., p. 7.
48. Michael Schudson, *Advertising, the Uneasy Persuasion* (New York: Basic Books, Inc.), 1984.
49. Ibid., p. 210.
50. Ibid., p. 214.
51. Ibid., p. 215.
52. Ibid.
53. Ibid., p. 218.
54. Ibid., p. 221.
55. Ibid., p. 210.
56. Ibid., p. 227. (Herbert Krugman, articulator of the low-involvement learning approach to television advertising.)
57. Ibid., p. 231.
58. Ibid., p. 232.
59. Ibid.
60. Ibid., p. 233.
61. Ibid. Emphasis in original.
62. Ibid., p. 232.
63. Ibid., p. 233. Emphasis in original.

Part 2

Issues
of
Consequence

Chapter 5

Advertising and the Economic Dimension

Why have so many studied the economic effects of advertising for such a long period of time? The reasons are probably quite simple:

1. Advertising is a major industry in the United States, with over $70 billion spent annually.
2. Advertising is a highly visible institution, its messages touching almost everyone every day.
3. There is a common belief among many business people that advertising "sells" the product or service. If sales are down, the blame is laid on advertising; if sales are increasing, advertising gets the credit.

BASIC LIMITATIONS OF MANY ECONOMIC STUDIES

Before beginning a discussion of some of the issues concerning the economic effects of advertising, it is necessary to look at some basic underpinnings of many economic studies related to advertising. In many of the studies, there is an implicit assumption that advertising works in isolation rather than in concert with other elements of the marketing mix (product, place, price, and promotion) and the promotion mix (advertising, personal selling, sales promotion, and public relations). However, if one examines expenditure patterns within the promotion mix, for example, it becomes clear that examining just advertising expenditures can lead to erroneous results. Compared with the over $70 billion spent annually on advertising, business firms spend approximately $150 billion on personal selling[1] and approximately $30 billion on sales promotion efforts.[2] It is difficult to imagine that anything but a synergistic effect on sales could be expected from the combination of the marketing and promotion mixes.

Other studies fail to take account of the many external factors that influence the effectiveness of a firm's advertising. For example, the advertising and promotion activities of competitors can dramatically affect a firm's advertising effectiveness.

Another critical factor often ignored in studies attempting to determine the economic effects of advertising is the cooperative advertising allowance made to retailers. Young has reported that "for many household items, over one-half of all retail advertising is sponsored by some type of cooperative funding."[3]

An additional handicap to research into the economic effects of advertising was pointed out by Morgenstern, who found that necessary data are often unavailable and, when available, are often inaccurate or untrustworthy.[4] For example, the industry classifications used in government data may group together firms producing unrelated products, or firms may switch classifications without any change in the kinds of goods they produce.[5]

It is also unlikely that individual firms over time or firms within a particular industry are equally effective in the development and transmission of their advertising.[6] Not all copy platforms, basic research programs, or media strategies are equally productive.

Lastly, few scholars in the economics area are conversant with basic material on consumer behavior such as that presented in Chapter 6 of this book, "Advertising and Its Audience." Definitions of what is information or how it is processed by the consumer are often ignored. In other instances, consumer behavior concepts are defined in a manner to suit a more "economic" view of the research process.

TWO SCHOOLS OF THOUGHT ABOUT THE ECONOMIC EFFECTS OF ADVERTISING

Albion indicates there are two principal models that economists use to describe the effects of advertising: the advertising = market power school and the advertising = market competition school. The first model views advertising as a persuasive communications tool that marketers use to make consumers less sensitive to price. This decreased price sensitivity will subsequently increase the firm's market power. The second model regards advertising as informative in nature and contends that it increases consumers' price sensitivity and stimulates competition among firms.[7]

The market power school believes advertising is capable of changing consumer tastes and building brand loyalty. A brand-loyal customer is not very price sensitive, as he/she does not perceive that there are acceptable alternatives in the marketplace. Once the firm has been able to differentiate its product/service through advertising expenditures, the firm should be able to increase its prices to consumers, subsequently increasing its profits and reducing competition in the marketplace.

The market competition model holds that advertising provides basic information to the marketplace, information that will increase price sensitivity, lower prices, and reduce any potential monopoly power. Ornstein described the market competition model as follows:

> The essence of this new view is that advertising provides information on brands, prices, and quality, thus increasing buyer knowledge, reducing consumers' search costs, and reducing the total costs to society of transacting business. By increasing information, advertising increases the number of substitutes known to buyers, thereby increasing price elasticity of demand and reducing price-cost margins. Far from being a barrier to entry, advertising facilitates entry by allowing previously unknown products to gain rapid market acceptance. . . . Advertising serves consumers by increasing product variety and by permitting firms to exploit economies of scale in production and distribution—which in turn yield lower consumer prices.[8]

Table 5-1 summarizes the two approaches.

These two approaches have some major flaws. As discussed by Albion,[9] the market power model assumes that advertising is probably the sole cause of brand loyalty and price insensitivity. But there are other elements in the marketing mix or promotion mix such as packaging, better product quality, personal selling, and sales promotion that could contribute to the development of brand loyalty. The market competition school assumes that consumers engage in a thorough and extensive search of product/service alternatives which is facilitated by advertising. The school also assumes that consumers are excellent judges of the merits of competing brands. Given our discussion in Chapter 7, this assumption does not necessarily hold.

SOME NEWER APPROACHES

Porter and Steiner have each developed new approaches to studying the economic effects of advertising. The main contribution of these two models has been to recognize the role of the retailer in both the sale of and the dissemination of information about the manufacturer's product to the ultimate consumer.

TABLE 5-1
Two Schools of Thought on the Role of Advertising in the Economy

ADVERTISING = MARKET POWER		ADVERTISING = MARKET COMPETITION
Advertising affects consumer preferences and tastes, changes product attributes, and differentiates the product from competitive offerings.	Advertising	Advertising informs consumers about product attributes and does not change the way they value these attributes
Consumers become brand loyal and less price sensitive, and perceive fewer substitutes for advertised brands.	Consumer Buying Behavior	Consumers become more price sensitive and buy best "value." Only the relationship between price and quality affects elasticity for a given product.
Potential entrants must overcome established brand loyalty and spend relatively more on advertising	Barriers to Entry	Advertising makes entry possible for new brands because it can communicate product attributes to consumers.
Firms are insulated from market competition and potential rivals; concentration increases, leaving firms with more discretionary power.	Industry Structure and Market Power	Consumers can compare competitive offerings easily and competitive rivalry is increased. Efficient firms remain, and as the inefficient leave, new entrants appear; the effect on concentration is ambiguous.
Firms can charge higher prices and are not as likely to compete on quality or price dimensions. Innovation may be reduced.	Market Conduct	More informed consumers put pressure on firms to lower prices and improve quality. Innovation is facilitated via new entrants.
High prices and excessive profits accrue to advertisers and give them even more incentive to advertise their products. Output is restricted compared to conditions of perfect competition.	Market Performance	Industry prices are decreased. The effect on profits due to increased competition and an increase in efficiency is ambiguous.

Reprinted with permission of the publisher from Mark S. Albion, *Advertising's Hidden Effects: Manufacturers' Advertising and Retail Pricing* (Boston, Mass.: Auburn House, 1983), p. 18.

Porter divides retail goods into two sectors, convenience and nonconvenience. Convenience goods retailers (gasoline stations, convenience food stores, traditional supermarkets) provide display space for the manufacturer's product, but that is about the only service they offer. The manufacturer has already differentiated the product with the advertising to create demand and eventually develop brand loyalty among consumers. The manufacturer subsequently increases prices to the retailer, thereby reducing trade margins. Retailers will be willing to accept price increases because of higher product turnover. Consumers engage in limited information search because of the low cost of these items.[10]

Nonconvenience goods retailers (auto dealers, appliance stores, furniture stores) play a more significant marketing role. The retailer is often asked to provide information about the product, to demonstrate it, and relate it to the store's image. More manufacturer advertising dollars are spent promoting the product to the trade (push strategy) in order to gain additional outlets. Consumers spend more time looking for the "best buy." The brand name, developed through manufacturer advertising, may not be all-important; store advertising and cooperative advertising may be just as important. As a result, manufacturer prices may be lower to maintain distribution in critical stores.[11]

The contributions of this model are clear. It stipulates that studying the economic effects of advertising is at best situational (convenience vs. nonconvenience goods) and that advertising as economists generally study it may be more important for the convenience goods sector. It also involves the retailer as an important element in the system.

Steiner's dual-stage model also indicates that the retailer must be viewed as an integral part of the economics of advertising.[12] A scenario for Steiner's model would be as follows:

In the early stages of a product, it is generally unadvertised, and consumers exhibit no particular preference among a wide variety of close substitutes. Then as Steiner describes the process:

> If a dealer in an unadvertised product category carries, say, 5 to 6 items, he is likely to be offered 100 by the manufacturers and finds he can select and substitute between them quite freely without a noticeable impact on his sales volume. As the retailer puts it, he can live without virtually any manufacturer product. Consequently, he plays one maker off against the next and ends up carrying the factory brands that afford him the greatest margin between retail list and factory invoice price. This causes factory demand curves to be extremely elastic and price to be depressed close to average unit cost.[13]

Consumer prices may well remain high because of the lack of competition at the retail level.

If now Manufacturer X begins successfully to advertise his brand, the terms of trade shift decisively in his favor. Dealers find the public expects them to handle the item. Hence, the trade's ability to stock a competing article in place of Brand X or to beat down the latter's price as a condition for carrying it is substantially diminshed. As advertising expands the popularity of Brand X, its maker therefore finds he can increase its retail distribution with progressively fewer price concessions.[14]

Consumer prices may fall because of the increased competition at the retail level. Intense price competition could follow, driving retail margins to the new zero level, as retailers begin offering heavy discounts on the items or offer them as loss leaders to generate store traffic. Retailers will use these heavily advertised products in this way because consumers tend to use them as benchmarks in price comparisons. Factory prices at this stage might remain relatively constant or even increase.

At this point, Steiner indicates that one of three situations will probably occur:[15]

1. Manufacturer's brand domination
2. Mixed regimen
3. Private label domination

In the case of manufacturer's brand domination, it is possible that, from the point of view of the market power school, the heavily advertised brands will dominate the market and thus create major barriers to entry by new firms. Those controlling the market may see opportunities to offer a variety of new brands and advertise them heavily. Product differences would be relatively minor. Consumer prices would rise given the successful new differentiation effort. The aspirin and detergent markets might be good examples of this situation.

In the mixed regimen situation, private labels may develop as the retailer attempts to challenge the manufacturers to restore some of their gross margins. Retailers can often negotiate low manufacturer prices for their own labels because manufacturers want to put excess plant capacity to use. The resulting competition between private and national brands keeps factory and consumer prices of national brands at reasonable levels. The retail prices of the advertised brands are lower than prices would be without advertising because of the continual low gross margins earned by retailers. The replacement tire market is an example of this situation, with 50 percent of the market being held by private labels. Many of the traditional canned goods in supermarkets probably also follow this scenario.

Few examples of the private label domination situation can be cited. If this situation did exist, it would mean high margins for retailers and consumer prices slightly below prices found when there is manufacturer's brand domination but above those in the mixed regimen.

In Steiner's model advertising can be seen as increasing distribution and thus potential users while diminishing the gross margin earned by retailers. At the same time, it allows factory prices to increase more than consumer prices.[16]

THE BASIC
ECONOMIC ISSUES

As the basic economic issues are reviewed, it will become evident that the phrase "It depends" will play an important role. Often, only mixed conclusions will be reached for many of the issue areas. These mixed conclusions probably arise from the limitations discussed earlier in this chapter—viewing advertising as an isolated function, using inaccurate data, etc.—or from failing to recognize the thrust of the Porter and Steiner models.

Advertising and Price

Does advertising lead to lower prices or does it make items the consumer purchases more expensive? Before the price question can be answered, as Norris indicates, one must inquire about what kind of advertising is being discussed, retail or national.[17] His distinction between national and retail advertising is the same one that Porter and Steiner have made.

A number of studies have indicated that high levels of retail advertising increase price competition and may subsequently lower relative consumer brand prices.[18] Product groups including gasoline, drugs, eyeglasses, and eye care are often cited as examples. As for national advertising, Norris concluded in his review of the economics literature that national advertising probably raises the price of goods and services.[19] Studies by Comanor and Wilson[20] and Lambin[21] concluded that advertising decreases factory price sensitivity. The factory price vs. consumer price (retail price) conclusions of these studies seem to be in agreement with the assumptions of both the Porter and the Steiner models.

Economies of Scale

Concerning scale economies (for example, a doubling of inputs may yield an output that is more than doubled) in advertising, there seems to be a mixed set of results. Many economists and marketers have assumed that there are increasing returns to advertising expenditures. A campaign must reach a certain level of expenditure to generate the most efficient level of response.[22] It is assumed that large firms can more easily reach this level of response than can firms with more limited resources.

Economies of scale in advertising can occur because there is a threshold of awareness that advertising must cross. Though it is assumed that a certain amount of message repetition is necessary before consumers become aware of a product or service, unfortunately no one knows exactly what that threshold is. The exact amount of message repetition needed to communicate effectively to consumers is often a function of such factors as risk, novelty, perceived differences in product alternatives, degree of confidence about a purchase, and the type of decision-making rules consumers employ (see Chapter 6). If a high rate of repetition is required, many smaller firms could be excluded because they lack a substantial promotion budget.

Can larger firms produce "better" advertising? Through the use of marketing research and copy-testing procedures combined with the excellent creative departments at major advertising agencies, it may be possible for the larger advertiser to produce more "effective" advertisements. No studies that the authors are familiar with have been conducted in this area.

Evidence that larger advertisers receive dramatically different media discounts than smaller advertisers is also lacking.[23] Although such differentials did apparently occur as late as the 1970s, the differentials now seem rather small.

Advertising's Effects on Profits

Conclusions regarding the effect of advertising on profits are clouded by measurement problems, cause-and-effect issues, and definitions of basic terms. Some authors have concluded that advertising has little effect on profit rates,[24] while others have found that advertising leads to higher profit rates.[25] Because of these confusing results, researchers have often turned to another measure of the market power of advertising, concentration.

Advertising and Concentration

The concentration ratio which has been used in most of the studies in this area of research is based upon a ranking of the firms in an industry by order of size (usually sales or employees) starting from the largest. The percentage of each firm's sales to the total industry sales is first derived. Then the top X firms' percentages are added to obtain a concentration ratio. Published statistics usually give concentration ratios for the largest 4, largest 8, and sometimes the largest 20 firms in the industry.[26]

It is assumed, especially by the market power school, that advertising expenditures are related to these measures of market concentration. Advertising would cause these high concentration levels because:

1. Economies of scale in advertising would enable large-scale advertisers to push smaller advertisers out of the market.
2. Increased capital requirements and brand loyalty would discourage potential entrants.[27]

Norris indicates that the trend of increased concentration in this country has been much more severe in some industries than in others. Between 1947 and 1963, the number of firms increased in 64 percent of producer goods industries and decreased in 33 percent. In consumer goods industries, the number of firms increased in only 33 percent but decreased in 67 percent. Within this consumer goods sector, Norris also states that the number of firms decreased in 57 percent of the industries in which brands are only slightly differentiated but decreased 88 percent in the highly differentiated industries.[28]

Scherer,[29] Mann,[30] Blair,[31] Lancaster et al.,[32] and Mueller[33] found that advertising inequalities explain the largest share of the variance in market concentration. Many of these studies found the electronic media, especially television, to be a prime factor in leading to increased levels of concentration. However, Comanor and Wilson,[34] Albion,[35] Ornstein and Lustgarten,[36] and Vernon[37] found no significant relationships between advertising and concentration. An interesting finding by Caves et al. was that advertising was highest in medium concentrated industries and lower in high and low concentrated industries.[38]

Norris would conclude that advertising does lead to higher levels of concentration in consumer goods industries.[39] There is, however, enough mixed evidence to indicate that the relationship may not be so simple. Again, there are probably specific industries and situations when advertising can lead to higher levels of concentration, but a sweeping statement that advertising always develops concentration may not be possible at this time.

Advertising and Aggregate Consumption

Several studies have investigated the effect of advertising on aggregate consumption. Schmalensee found high correlations between advertising and aggregate consumption, correlations that were improved when advertising was moved from cause (preceding consumption) to effect (lagging behind consumption).[40] He points out, however, that in spite of an increase in the ratio of advertising to GNP, the ratio of household spending to household disposable income has remained stable over the long term.[41] He concludes that national advertising does not affect total spending for goods and services.[42] Other researchers, however, disagree with Schmalensee. Indications that advertising does affect aggregate consumption have been reported by Taylor and Weiserbs[43] and Cowling et al.[44]

Most of the evidence would seem to indicate that advertising is the result rather than the cause of consumption. The conclusion that advertising does not increase aggregate consumption may be based on the way that advertising budgets are traditionally established at the manufacturers' level. Many firms continue to use a percentage-of-sales method, which will always view sales as the cause of advertising rather than as the result. Also, the studies on aggregate consumption have made an implicit assumption that advertising affects consumer attitudes and values concerning their saving and spending patterns. Yet none of the studies have explored this underlying assumption. The two confounding factors introduced above can only lead to the conclusion that it simply is not clear whether advertising affects aggregate consumption patterns.

Advertising's Effect on Primary Demand

Primary demand is the demand for all the brands, advertised or unadvertised, within a given product category. Borden's 1942 study concluded:

> [So far as primary demand is concerned] from the many cases analyzed and from the industry studies, one clear and important generalization can be made, namely, that basic trends of demand for products, which are determined by underlying social and environmental conditions, are more significant in determining the expansion or contraction of primary demand than is the use or lack of use of advertising.[45]

Grabowski concluded that "the main impact of advertising is on a consumer's choice of brands or products within a particular class rather than across product classes."[46] Lambin probably best critiqued knowledge in this area: "In only four product markets out of ten have statistically significant (barely, at low levels) industry advertising effects been observed on primary demand. . . . Those four product classes are all in the early stages of the life cycle, where product-related social, economic, and technological forces are favorable to the spontaneous expansion of demand."[47]

The finding that advertising can speed growth rates (not cause dramatic shifting between product categories) under favorable conditions within a given product category gives the critics of advertising another reason to condemn the institution. In fact, either a positive or negative finding in this area would lead advertising to be damned. If advertising simply leads consumers to change from one brand of aspirin to another or from one brand of dishwashing detergent to another, it is a social waste. If advertising does increase primary demand, then advertising "can quite easily be accused of being nothing more than an antisocial tool, the properties of which range from those of a propaganda device of Orwellian proportions, an uncontrolled, insidious, pervasive activity capable of changing consumers' 'desires' to the more academic ideas of Chamberlain and Galbraith that it is a means by which capitalist corporations control demand."[48]

SOME CONCLUSIONS

Is advertising a social waste or does it benefit society and the individual consumers who comprise that society? There is no firm answer to the question. As Norris states, "The most obvious and perhaps the only certain conclusion to be drawn from this plethora of studies is that there is manifold disagreement among the students of the economic effects of advertising."[49]

Chiplin and Sturgess underscore the point at the end of *Economics of Advertising*:

> Our discussions have indicated that there is no consensus in economics concerning the net benefit or cost of advertising to society. Much here depends on the value judgements of the particular individual. There are, therefore, no clear-cut policy recommendations. In the remainder of this chapter we shall discuss the forms of policy towards advertising that have been suggested, while leaving the reader to decide whether any or all of the policies are necessary and if so, the precise way in which they should be implemented.[50]

There is hope of finding more definitive results through the recent contributions made by Porter, Steiner, and Albion and Ferris. They have broadened the economic horizon by adding the retailer component, recognizing that there are different types of consumer goods, and explicitly recognizing the difference between demand at the retail and factory levels with regard to price. Advertising is here to stay; it is to be hoped that future research will provide better ways to refine this social institution.

Notes

1. Philip Kotler, *Marketing Management: Analysis, Planning, and Control* (Englewood Cliffs, N.J.: Prentice-Hall, 1984), p. 675.
2. Ibid., p. 660.
3. Robert F. Young, *Cooperative Advertising, Its Uses and Effectiveness: Some Preliminary Hypotheses*, Report No. 79-112 (Cambridge, Mass.: Marketing Science Institute, 1979), p. 5.
4. Oskar Morgenstern, *On the Accuracy of Economic Observations* (Princeton: Princeton University Press, 1963).
5. Richard Schmalensee. *The Economics of Advertising* (Amsterdam: North Holland Publishing Co., 1972), p. 146.
6. David Ogilvy and J. Raphaelson, "Research on Advertising Techniques That Work and Don't Work,"*Harvard Business Review* 60 (July/August, 1982), pp. 14-18.

7. Mark S. Albion, *Advertising's Hidden Effects: Manufacturers' Advertising and Retail Pricing* (Boston, Mass.: Auburn House, 1983), pp. 16-17.

8. S. I. Ornstein, *Industrial Concentration and Advertising Intensity* (Washington, D.C.: American Enterprise Institute, 1977), pp. 2-3.

9. Albion, op. cit., pp. 17-21.

10. Mark S. Albion and Paul W. Farris, *The Advertising Controversy: Evidence on the Economic Effects of Advertising* (Boston, Mass.: Auburn House, 1981), p. 139.

11. Ibid.

12. Ibid., pp. 144-145.

13. Robert Steiner, "A Dual Stage Approach to the Effects of Brand Advertising on Competition and Price," in *Marketing and the Public Interest*, ed. John Cady (Cambridge, Mass.: Marketing Science Institute, 1978), p. 131.

14. Ibid., p. 134.

15. Albion and Farris, op. cit., p. 148.

16. Ibid., p. 149.

17. Vincent P. Norris, "The Economic Effects of Advertising: A Review of the Literature," in *Current Issues of Research in Advertising*, ed. James H. Leigh and Claude Martin, Jr. (Ann Arbor: Division of Research, Graduate School of Business Administration, University of Michigan, 1984), p. 93.

18. See Norris, op. cit., pp. 93-94, and Albion and Farris, op. cit., p. 170.

19. Norris, op. cit., p. 105.

20. William S. Comanor and Thomas A. Wilson, *Advertising and Market Power* (Cambridge, Mass.: Harvard University Press, 1974).

21. J. J. Lambin, *Competition and Market Conduct in Oligopoly over Time* (Amsterdam: North Holland Publishing Co., 1976).

22. Albion and Farris, op. cit., p. 103.

23. John L. Peterman, "Differences Between the Levels of Spot and Network Advertising Rates," *Journal of Business*, 52(October, 1979), pp. 549-562.

24. See R. Ayanian, "Advertising and Rate of Return," *Journal of Law and Economics*, 18(October, 1975), pp. 479-501, and H. Block, "Advertising and Profitability: A Reappraisal," *Journal of Political Economy*, 82(March/April, 1974), pp. 267-286.

25. See Comanor and Wilson, op. cit., and John M. Vernon and Robert E. M. Nourse, "Profit Rates and Market Structure of Advertising Intensive Firms," *Journal of Industrial Economics*, 22(September, 1973), pp. 1-20.

26. Richard Caves, *American Industry: Structure, Conduct, Performance* (Englewood Cliffs, N.J.: Prentice-Hall, 1964), p. 8.

27. Albion and Farris, op. cit., p. 60.

28. Norris, op. cit., p. 88.

29. F. Scherer, *Industrial Market Structure and Economic Performance*, (Chicago: Rand McNally, 1980), ch. 14.

30. H. Mann, "Advertising, Concentration, and Profitability: The State of Knowledge and Directions for Public Policy," in *Economic Concentration, The New Learning*, ed. Harvey Goldschmid, H. Mann, and J. Weston (Boston: Little, Brown, 1974).

31. John Blair, *Economic Concentration: Structure, Behavior and Public Policy* (New York: Harcourt Brace Jovanovich, 1972), pp. 311, 321-331.

32. K. Lancaster, R. Batra, and G. Miracle, "How the Level, Intensity, and Distribution of Advertising Affect Market Concentration," in *Proceedings of the 1982 Conference of the American Academy of Advertising*, ed. Alan Fletcher (Lincoln, Nebr.: American Academy of Advertising, 1982).

33. W. Mueller, "Changes in Market Concentration of Manufacturing Industries 1946-1977," *Review of Industrial Concentration*, 1(Spring, 1984), pp. 1-14.

34. Comanor and Wilson, op. cit.

35. Mark S. Albion, "The Determinants of the Level of Advertising and Media Mix Expenditures in Consumer Goods Industries," unpublished manuscript, Harvard University, January, 1976.

36. Stanley I. Ornstein and Steven Lustgarten, "Advertising Intensity and Industrial Concentration—An Empirical Inquiry, 1947-1967," in *Issues in Advertising: The Economics of Persuasion*, ed. David G. Tueruck (Washington, D.C.: American Enterprise Institute for Public Policy Research, 1978), pp. 217-253.

37. John M. Vernon, "Concentration, Promoting, and Market Share Stability in the Pharmaceutical Industry," *Journal of Industrial Economics*, 19(July, 1971), pp. 146-266,

38. Richard E. Caves, Michael E. Porter, and A. Michael Spence, with John T. Scott, *Competition in the Open Economy* (Cambridge, Mass.: Harvard University Press, 1980).

39. Norris, op. cit., pp. 88-92.

40. Richard Schmalensee, "Advertising and Economic Welfare," in *Advertising and the Public Interest*, ed. S.F. Divita (Chicago: American Marketing Association, 1974), p. 266.

41. Ibid., p. 264.

42. Ibid., pp. 58, 85-86.

43. L. Taylor and D. Weiserbs, "Advertising and the Aggregate Consumption Function," *American Economic Review*, 62(September-December, 1971), pp. 642-655.

44. Keith Cowling et al., *Advertising and Economy Behavior* (London: Macmillan, 1975).

45. N. H. Borden, *The Economic Effects of Advertising* (Chicago: Irwin, 1942), p. 433.

46. H. Grabowski, "The Effects of Advertising on Intraindustry Shifts in Demand," *Explorations in Economic Research*: Occasional Papers of the National Bureau for Economic Research, 4(Winter, 1977-Spring, 1978), pp. 675-701.
47. Lambin, op. cit., p. 136.
48. P. Kyle, "The Impact of Advertising on Markets," *International Journal of Advertising*, 1(October-December, 1982), pp. 345-359.
49. Norris, op. cit., p. 116.
50. B. Chiplin and B. Sturgess, *Economics of Advertising* (London: Holt, Rinehart and Winston with the Advertising Association, 1981), p. 134.

Chapter 6

Advertising and Its Audience

This chapter will depart from many others written on the same topic. We will not discuss basic demographic characteristics of audiences, identify the types of consumers who tend to watch more televison, or include any of the wealth of information that syndicated services provide on media and product usage patterns.

Instead of focusing on the advertising audience in general terms, we will center our discussion on the concept of information. The views of Carey and Sandage, reviewed in Chapter 4, suggest that advertising is an institution that attempts to transmit different types of market information, information that presumably matches buyers and sellers in the marketplace. This information can be functional in nature, such as the amount of hot water that various kinds of dishwashers use. It can also be aesthetic or symbolic, such as whether a cologne or aftershave lotion suits the self-image of a consumer.

We will focus on the impact of advertising information on the individual consumer. By individual consumer, we mean the average consumer who must enter the marketplace to buy anything from salt to a new automobile. This definition excludes those who buy professionally for others—e.g., purchasing agents. These institutional buyers have been excluded because we wish to focus our discussion on typical consumer advertising. For it is here that advertising's role is most praised and damned.

Since this chapter will view advertising as an informational medium, we will see how individual consumers acquire information and subsequently evaluate it in order to make final purchase decisions. Advertising's role in the process will be examined as well. It is felt that this perspective offers potential for considerable understanding of the interaction between advertising and the individual.

THE BASIC
INFORMATIONAL
FUNCTIONS
OF ADVERTISING

Sheth believes that advertising fulfills four basic functions—precipitation, persuasion, reinforcement, and reminder.[1] *Precipitation* induces consumers to move from a state of indecision to one where purchase of a particular brand is a definite possibility. It attempts to intensify existing needs and wants. Its main function is to create general awareness and brand knowledge among large groups of potential customers.

When new products are introduced to the marketplace, there is usually an initial burst of advertising. The advertising usually indicates that a new product is available, tells something about its unique features, and indicates where it may be purchased. This is typical of the precipitation function.

Persuasion is seen as the mechanism by which advertising actually induces purchase. By using appeals to basic emotions such as love, hate, fear, or the need for self-esteem and/or appeals to reason, as in a factual summary of product attributes, it attempts to develop actual sales.

For example, advertisers of home security systems hope their messages reach those who have recently been victimized by crime or know of someone who has. By utilizing a strong appeal to fear, they attempt to get these potential consumers to move to an immediate purchase of the security system, based on their past disturbing experience with crime.

The *reinforcement* mechanism provides information that will legitimize *previous* choices. Information is given that indicates the wisdom of the existing choice or validates a previous decision to reject a particular product.

Automobile companies often do an excellent job of reinforcement advertising. Usually, after a new car has been purchased, the buyer is made a member of a special club formed by the company. Each month he/she receives a magazine that offers glowing information about the car just purchased.

Finally, the *reminder* mechanism is said to act as a triggering cue for habitual brand behavior (brand loyalty) learned from prior experiences and exposure to information. With products that are purchased frequently, customers need to be reminded about a particular brand because of the many conflicting messages they will hear about competing brands. The large volume of advertising done for the popular soft drinks and fast-food establishments is an example of reminder advertising.

Figure 6-1 demonstrates the sequential nature of the four advertising mechanisms. It is hypothesized that consumers move through these four mechanisms in making initial purchases. Not all consumers, however, will cycle completely through to the reminder stage. Some will remain at

FIGURE 6-1
Basic Advertising Mechanisms

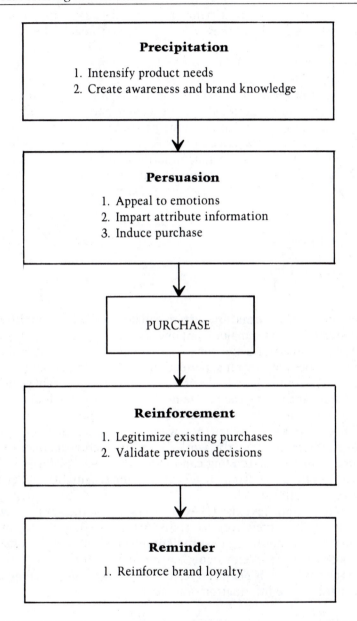

reinforcement. This usually occurs for infrequently purchased products such as autos and color television sets. Some consumers will become satiated or bored with an existing product. When satiation or boredom occurs, it is suggested that they will enter the first stage of the cycle again and begin to search for new product alternatives. For example, a homemaker may become "tired" of a sofa and seek to buy a new one, feeling it will "liven up" the living room.

The key to the Sheth model presumably is information. It seems apparent that the four functions are performed in part through advertising. The consumer can be seen as constantly in the marketplace for products and services. Thus, there is a constant sending and receiving of advertising information fulfilling various functions for both the consumer and the advertiser. This process, then, provides the impetus for the active exchange of goods and services in the marketplace.

THE "IMPERFECT" INFORMATION SYSTEM OF THE MARKETPLACE

The marketplace information system can be viewed in a simplified perspective as having two major components—advertisers and consumers. Matching of advertisers and consumers is based upon information. Yet, the market does not exhibit a "perfect" matching of buyers and sellers by objective standards. Hundreds of new products fail each year, retail outlets constantly have the problem of carrying too much of the wrong product (or too little of the right one), and consumers often complain that they are unable to find what they want at the price they wish to pay. Although the market clearly "works" in a satisfactory manner much of the time, some understanding can be gained by suggesting it still performs at less than an optimal level considering the quality and quantity of messages available. Why?

Several possibilities exist: (1) Advertisers are not transmitting *enough* information; (2) Advertisers are transmitting the *wrong* information; (3) Consumers do not *seek out* sufficient information; and (4) Consumers make poor decisions even when *given* adequate information.

On the basis of this perspective, let us now examine the components of the marketplace information system.

Advertisers

The information transmitted by advertisers is often of a persuasive nature. Since all advertisers attempt to present their products or services in the most favorable light, the information transmitted will not be perfectly objective. For example, cigarette manufacturers do not emphasize in their advertising the fact that smoking is dangerous to health. Nor do food product advertisers discuss the presence of certain additives in their products, as such a discussion could make the product less appealing.

Critics have often taken issue with the persuasive nature of advertising, claiming that it subverts the consumer's "rational" decision processes. But, as Borden has argued, "Whether one likes persuasion or not, it appears inevitable in a free society."[2] As Carey suggested, the persuasive nature of advertising communications is an institutionally understandable part of our market economy. The market economy basically presumes that firms will operate in their own self-interest to produce sales and profits; persuasive advertisements are thus a vehicle to achieve that end.

Closely related to the persuasion issue is the issue of frequency. Frequency is something that all consumers are aware of and many are annoyed by—the intrusive repetition of many commercial messages. Recognizing that their messages are among hundreds attempting to attract the attention of consumers, advertisers use the technique of repetition to attract their share of attention. They are trying to be "heard above the crowd."

Although advertisers view repetition as an important technique in selling products, they are often unsure about how much repetition to use. Sometimes an ad is repeated too many times and sometimes not repeated often enough. It is usually quite difficult to determine the optimal expenditure of media dollars.

Related to repetition is the issue of occasion—the time of day that an advertisement is presented. Many consumers complain about promotion of certain kinds of products at the dinner hour—laxatives or hemorrhoid preparations, for example. Again, however, the advertiser is presumably acting on self-interest. Large numbers of people are viewing television during the dinner hour, and many of these people are users or potential users of these products. Since advertisers want to reach as many potential customers as possible, they see the dinner hour as an ideal time for them to transmit their messages.

In addition to "puffing" their products, repeating their ads too often, or placing them at "inappropriate" times, advertisers may direct their messages to the wrong audience. The advertiser may have perceived the market to be the twenty- to thirty-year-old group when, in fact, the major market for the product is consumers forty to fifty years of age. This misdirected information may not effectively reach the "prime market" and consequently will be of little value to either advertiser or consumer.

At other times advertisers send messages that consumers do not understand, or interpret incorrectly. For example, consumers may have seen an ad for a paint sale at a local hardware store. The ad may have failed to state clearly enough that only certain colors were on sale, leaving some consumers with the impression that the sale prices applied to all colors of paint. The subsequent visit to the hardware store will prove unsatisfactory for both the advertiser and the consumer.

In sum, advertisers do not always transmit "perfect" information for either their own or the consumer's interests. Because of practices such as attempting to induce purchase through partial information, making mistakes in frequency rates and timing, developing poor messages, and transmitting information to the wrong audience, less than optimal information may be offered by advertisers to consumers.

Consumers

Consumers, as well, are "imperfect" in the way they go about gathering and processing information. They are not the rational people that classical economists had hoped they were. Although there is evidence that consumers approach some buying decisions in a deliberate manner, there is also good reason to believe that a good deal of purchasing behavior involves little conscious decision making.

Much decision making does not follow the systematic approaches presented in formal consumer behavior models. Rarely does a consumer proceed smoothly from need recognition, to information acquisition, to purchase. The decision process may take place over a long period of time with incomplete and often ambiguous data, and the final decision may be made with something less than total confidence.[3]

A consumer's ability to process bits of information is also imperfect. At any given time, individuals can probably actively process only a limited amount of information.[4] When the buying environment is very complex, it is easy to become "overloaded" with information. Take, for example, the process of deciding what house to buy. After looking at many different houses and collecting a myriad of data, how many consumers base their final decision on an essentially minor feature, such as whether a fence is part of the property? For some home buyers, the mass of information about unique support features, insulation, wiring, landscaping, fireplaces, size of lot, and heating and cooling systems can be too much to deal with.

Consumer behavior is aptly described in March and Simon's concept of "bounded rationality": Faced with a very complex environment and limited resources (time, money, cognitive capabilities), consumers attempt to resolve buying problems in ways that are satisfactory rather than optimal.[5] In Bauer's view of consumer behavior, "Consumers characteristically develop decision strategies and ways of reducing risk that enable them to act with relative confidence and ease in situations where their information is inadequate and the consequences of their actions are in some meaningful sense incalculable."[6]

Thus, it appears that neither consumers nor advertisers always operate in an optimal manner in the marketplace. Yet, given this less than ideal performance on the part of both major components of the market information system, it is interesting to note that the system continues to function and has given apparently adequate service to many consumers and advertisers. The *perfect* marketplace has never existed—and never will. That does not mean, of course, that it is fruitless to search for ways to improve the existing mechanism.

One approach may be to look more closely at exactly *how* consumers use the information available to make buying decisions. Given some kind of descriptive model, it may be possible to better understand the "human" workings of the market, and thus be more adequately equipped to offer suggestions for improvement.

HOW CONSUMERS GATHER AND PROCESS INFORMATION

Of course consumers do not rely solely upon advertising to gather product brand information. There are five primary sources of information, both internal and external, available to consumers:[7]

1. *Memory*, of past searches, personal experiences, and low-involvement learning (internal information).
2. *Market-dominated sources* such as advertising, personal selling, etc.
3. *Consumer-dominated sources* such as family and friends.
4. *Neutral sources* such as *Consumer Reports* and various state and local government publications.
5. *Experiential sources* such as inspection or product trial.

These sources are shown in Figure 6-2.

When Are These Information Sources Used?

The internal information sources are the primary ones used by consumers, especially in cases where the consumer is involved in a very limited problem-solving situation or is brand loyal.[8] Mass media or market-dominated sources have been found to be important in the early stages of the decision process, when the buyer is informing himself/herself about possible alternatives (Sheth's precipitation function).[9] As the consumer nears a decision (Sheth's persuasion function), there is a tendency for consumers to use consumer-dominated sources.[10] Although little research has been done concerning Sheth's reinforcement and re-

FIGURE 6-2
Information Sources for a Purchase Decision

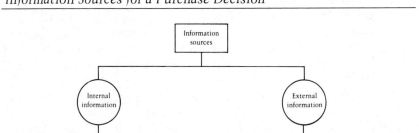

Source: Adapted from H. Beales, M. B. Mazis, S. C. Salop, and R. Staelin, "Consumer Search and Public Policy," *Journal of Consumer Research*, June, 1981, p. 12.

minder functions, it is reasonable to predict that some combination of internal and market-dominated sources is used.

There has been some research on the effect of product characteristics on information sources used. Research on the diffusion of information indicates that there is a tendency for buyers of new and high-involvement products to prefer consumer-dominated sources.[11] Settle found that for complex and socially visible products the preferred sources of information were conversations with experts and close friends. For durable and multipurpose products, the preferred information source was personal experience.[12]

The neutral channels are vastly underutilized. One study found 6 percent or less of female consumers utilizing neutral sources in the purchase of small appliances, clothing, and food items,[13] while other researchers found that neutral sources were valued sixth (out of six choices) in importance in the purchase of men's shirts and television sets.[14] It may be that many consumers are simply too lazy to seek out this information or, given the affluence of many consumers, may not consider it worth the time and effort. If a poor purchase is made, there are more funds available to correct the problem. It is clear that consumers rarely rely on a single source of information. These multiple information sources are complementary rather than competitive, and their use depends upon the situation in which the consumer finds himself or herself.

However, no matter which channel(s) the consumer uses, there still must be some motivation to gather information. The next section will deal with these motivating forces. Attempting to determine how consumers actually gain and process information is extremely complicated. We will attempt to first isolate some major concepts and then use them to guide our discussion.

What Motivates Consumers to Seek Information?

Let us first turn to some of the basic reasons why consumers seek information before making a purchase. Six major factors account for much of the information-seeking activity: perceived risk, novelty, greater differences in product alternatives, greater product importance, degree of confidence, and the involuntary situation—i.e., the need to replace an essential product or service.

RISK. In every buying decision, consumers have identified (however vaguely) a need and a product or service that will satisfy that need. Many buying decisions involve some perceived risk: as Bauer puts it, "Consumer behavior involves risk in the sense that any action of a consumer will produce consequences which he cannot anticipate with any approximate certainty."[15] How many times have we thought about buying something and yet been very unsure what purchase would be most satisfactory for the money involved?

Perceived risk is apparently a function of at least two factors—uncertainty and consequences.[16] Consumers may be uncertain about their goals. For example, a consumer who has identified the need for a new car might be unsure whether economy or comfort is a more important goal. Even if the consumer has established economy as the basic goal, there is still uncertainty about exactly what type of car will be best. A Ford Escort? A Honda? Thus, uncertainty deals with basic buying goals (economy vs. comfort) as well as with final specification of an exact product (Escort vs. Honda) that will satisfy the overall goal.

The consequences of a purchase are a second factor which can generate perceived risk. Consequences can be defined as "the amount that would be lost if the consequences of the act were not favorable.[17] If you buy the Escort, will it impress your friends as you hoped? You may also have had certain expectations of how well the Escort would perform. For example, you may be fearful that the maintenance record will not be as good as you might expect. The major types of risk that consumers may perceive in making product/service decisions have been categorized as follows:

1. FUNCTIONAL RISK. The product/service will not perform as expected. "Will the Honda get excellent highway gas mileage?"

2. PHYSICAL RISK. Using the product will involve risk to oneself or others. "Will the lawnmower be safe for my teenage son to operate?"
3. FINANCIAL RISK. The product/service will not be worth its cost in terms of money or time to acquire it. "Will driving to New York City from New Jersey to get a new VCR be worth it?"
4. SOCIAL RISK. The product/service will be an embarrassment to oneself. "Will others like my new entertainment center?"
5. PSYCHOLOGICAL RISK. The consumer's final choice will bruise the ego. "Will I really be happy in this apartment?"[18]

Taking the perspective suggested, then, consumers can reduce perceived risk by (a) decreasing uncertainty through information acquisition or (b) reducing the amount at stake. Some major risk-reduction or risk-avoidance strategies include the following:[19]

1. Information seeking from memory or market, consumer, or neutral dominated sources of information.
2. Development of brand loyalty toward a product/service instead of purchasing new or untried products/services.
3. Trusting of well-known brand names when experience has been minor in a product category (brand image).
4. Trusting of stores to provide only good-quality products/services (store image).
5. Choosing of the most expensive item.
6. Reliance upon private laboratory tests, money-back guarantees, warranties, and prepurchase trial (reassurance).

One researcher found that of the above risk-reduction strategies the ones preferred by consumers were developing brand loyalty and trusting brand images. The least preferred were buying the most expensive model and relying on private laboratory tests, money-back guarantees, and warranties.[20]

Reducing the consequences (the amount at stake) of a decision is a somewhat more difficult strategy to follow for most consumers than reducing uncertainty. To use our earlier example, it may be very difficult for a man to say that he does not care what his friends think of his new Escort if social esteem is important to him. It would also be difficult for him to minimize a poor maintenance record when it has cost him dearly to make repairs. Therefore, it appears more likely that consumers will tend to seek to reduce uncertainty through information acquisition or to avoid the uncertainty altogether.

The impression should not be left that all consumers act to reduce or avoid risk. Different individuals have different levels of tolerance for risk, each acting to reduce risk to a personally acceptable level. Certain consumers, in fact, have been found to act in a way that increases risk.[21] The Sheth model, discussed earlier, indicated that consumers who become satiated or bored by a product will accept the risk involved in seeking new product alternatives. Thus, consumers can have two entirely different strategies concerning risk. Whether they act to reduce it or to increase it, however, information acquisition plays a key role.

NOVELTY. Novelty is a second factor that motivates consumers to seek information.[22] All dimensions of newness in the market, such as new products or new advertising (appeals, media) can be viewed as stimuli that will motivate consumers to seek information. For many consumers, novelty is a change of pace from the usual way of doing things and thus holds intrinsic appeal. The new safer tire, the newly designed auto, or the unusual advertisement may all attract the initial attention of the consumer. Quite often the consumer will attempt to find out more with the possibility of eventually buying. The novelty factor, then, is clearly related to the situation in which consumers act to increase risk, as just discussed.

GREATER DIFFERENCES IN PRODUCT ALTERNATIVES. In a study of furniture and appliance purchases, Claxton et al. found that consumers who saw significant differences between brands visited more stores before making a buying decision.[23] Dissimilarities in product/service attributes may lead consumers to perceive substantial benefits from searching for information. Such benefits may not be as evident when products and services are perceived as "parity" or similar.

GREATER PRODUCT IMPORTANCE. Jacoby et al. found that the more important the product is to the consumer, the more thorough will be the search for information about it.[24] Moore and Lehmann found that the consumer's search for information was greater for the most important brand attributes.[25]

DEGREE OF CONFIDENCE. If consumers are confident about a purchase, they are not likely to seek much information. An example would be a consumer who is loyal to a particular brand of coffee. When coffee is on the grocery list, a favorite brand is automatically chosen from the supermarket shelf. Because of previous satisfactory experience with the brand, there is no motivation to seek information about the purchase. Conversely, a consumer who is not confident about a purchase (e.g., buying a home computer for the first time) will probably seek information about both the product class and the brands available.

Moore and Lehmann found that the greater the number of previous purchases, the less the information required.[26] However, Bennett and Mandell found that past experience with a product reduces the need for information only as long as the consumer is satisfied with the product.[27]

It may be that confidence and risk are closely related. If the consumer is very confident about an upcoming purchase, it may also be that little or no risk is perceived. Thus, in either instance, little information seeking will occur.

INVOLUNTARY SITUATION. A sixth and final factor that motivates information seeking is the involuntary situation. When the refrigerator or stove breaks for the last time, consumers are forced into the marketplace to gather information.

Given these six motivations for information seeking, we shall attempt to review some of the factors that affect *how much* information consumers will gather.

How Much Information Do Consumers Gather?

We do know that consumers are active in the marketplace in terms of gathering information. Often, however, the amount of information that *could* be gathered and processed is overwhelming. For example, on any drugstore shelf there are a dozen or more brands of shampoo. Each has a different price, different ingredients, different functions (for dry, normal, or oily hair, for dandruff, for body), and different quality-price associations. Information is readily available on the shampoo package and from prior learning about the products through advertisements and personal experience. Friends may have offered advice on what products are good. Hence, with little effort, the consumer can be exposed to a plethora of valuable product information.

Although the amount of external search that consumers undertake before making a purchase has been measured in a number of ways in the literature (number of stores visited, number of information sources consulted, number of alternatives considered, number of different types of information used, and time duration of the purchase decision), it is clear that for most consumers the amount of external research conducted is very limited. Dommermuth found that 36 percent of buyers considered only one brand of refrigerator and visited only one store before making a purchase.

For electric irons, the figure rose to 62 percent.[28] Hawkins et al.[29] suggest that buyers can be classified into three groups in terms of the search they engage in before making a major durable purchase:

1. NONSEARCHERS. They conduct little or no search prior to purchase (60%).
2. SEARCHERS. They are "thorough and balanced" in that they collect data from about three sources and visit about four stores (30%).

3. EXTENDED INFORMATION SEARCHERS. They acquire large
    amounts of information over a period of time (10%).

The amount of external search is also influenced by the nature of the
consumer. Information seekers represent the upper socioeconomic stra-
tum. They are generally better educated and more affluent, and they tend
to avail themselves of a wide range of information sources.[30]

A note of caution is appropriate here. It would appear from the following studies that many consumers, because they conduct no external
search, infrequently engage in a decision-making process before purchase. What these studies fail to note is the amount of internal search
(memory) each consumer engages in prior to making a purchase.[31] Little
is known about how this internal search is conducted.

Other equally important factors are the time and money it takes to
gather information. How many times have we bought the first item we
saw because we simply did not have the time or inclination to "look
around"? We may have known about a store that offered the same product
at a better price, but it was "just too far away." Thus, in many instances
information is not sought by consumers because the added costs of
search (time and money) are too high in light of the expected benefits this
information will provide for making a final decision.[32] Visiting few stores
and reviewing only a few brands may also indicate that consumers have
various decision-making rules that immediately limit their set of store
and brand alternatives.

Decision-Making Rules
That Consumers Use

Consumers often use decision-making rules when they attempt to evaluate and select alternatives they have discovered in the search process.
Some consumers average out some of the very good features with some of
the less attractive features of a product in determining overall brand
preference. The brand that rates highest on the sum of the consumer's
judgment of the relevant evaluative criteria will be chosen. This is
known as the linear compensatory rule.[33] This form of decision making
appears to be used in more complex high-involvement situations.

The following rules are called noncompensatory since very good performance on one evaluative criterion cannot compensate for poor performance on another evaluative criterion:

1. THE DISJUNCTIVE RULE. This rule establishes a minimum level of
    desired performance for each relevant attribute. The number of at-
    tributes will be small and the level of desired performance will gen-
    erally be high. All brands that surpass the performance for any at-
    tribute are considered acceptable. The consumer would say, "I'll

consider all (or buy the first) brands that perform really well on any attribute I consider to be important."[34]

2. THE CONJUNCTIVE RULE. A consumer will consider a brand only if it meets acceptable standards on all key attributes. If the washing machine meets the consumer's requirements for amount of water utilized and permanent-press features but is above a set limit on cost, it will be eliminated from the alternatives.[35]

3. THE LEXICOGRAPHIC RULE. The consumer rank-orders all the key brand attributes in terms of their perceived importance. After comparing the brands on the most important attributes, the one that is highest is selected. If there is a tie, brands are then evaluated on the second most important attribute.[36]

Certainly these are not the only decision-making rules that consumers employ. For many purchase situations, prior learning as a result of product trial may be utilized. Assessment of attributes may not be important and the consumer may choose the brand with the best overall impression. Schiffman and Kanuk call this the affect referred rule.[37]

Consumers may use only one rule or combine them in a myriad of ways to reach final purchase decisions. Low-involvement purchases probably involve simple decision-making rules such as the conjunctive, the disjunctive, or the lexicographic, since consumers may attempt to minimize the mental cost of such decisions.[38] High-involvement decisions may utilize complex rules such as the compensatory and may involve different rules at different stages of the decision-making process.[39] Although the use of these rules may reduce external search, it does not reduce the rationality of the consumer's decision-making process. Table 6-1 may help to clarify the above discussion.

How Does Information Influence Purchase?

There are many conflicting views of how information can influence a purchase decision. We shall review four views that have received some support from a host of studies conducted in the area. The approaches to be discussed view the influence process as occurring through the interaction of cognitive, affective, and conative elements. The cognitive component includes attention, awareness, comprehension, learning, interest, and beliefs; the affective component is concerned with interest, feeling, and evaluation; the conative factor deals with intentions to behave in a particular way—trial, action, and adoption.

THE LEARNING HIERARCHY. One view of the process, the learning hierarchy, states that information transmitted and subsequently gathered by consumers must first create changes in the cognitive component (awareness, attention, comprehension). In other words, the consumer

TABLE 6-1
Use of Decision-Making Rules in Choosing a Brand of Automobile

RULE	VERBAL DESCRIPTION	PERCENTAGE USING RULE
Disjunctive	I chose the car that had a really good rating on at least one characteristic.	0%
Conjunctive	I chose the car that didn't have any bad ratings.	0.6%
Lexicographic	I looked at the characteristic that was most important to me and chose the car that was best in that characteristic. If two or more of the cars were equal on that characteristic, I then looked at my second most important characteristic to break the tie.	60.7%
Compensatory	I chose the car that had a really good rating when you balanced the good ratings with the bad ratings.	32.1%
Disjunctive-conjunctive	I first eliminated any car that didn't have at least one really good score and then chose from the rest the product that didn't have a really bad score on any characteristic.	0%
Conjunctive-disjunctive	I first eliminated the cars with a bad rating on any characteristic and then chose from the rest the one with a high score on any characteristic.	0%
Disjunctive-compensatory	I first eliminated any car that didn't have at least one really good rating and then chose from the rest of the cars that seemed the best when you balanced the good ratings.	1.1%
Conjunctive-compensatory	I first eliminated the cars with a really bad rating on any characteristic and then chose from the rest the one that seemed the best overall when you balanced the good ratings with the bad ratings.	5.4%

Source: Derived from M. Reily and R. Holman, "Does Task Complexity or Cue Intercorrelation Affect Choice of an Information Processing Strategy: An Empirical Investigation," in *Advances in Consumer Research* IV, ed. W. D. Perrault, Jr. (Chicago: Association for Consumer Research, 1977), p. 189.

must first attend to and understand the information. If this is successfully accomplished, then changes in the affective component (attitude) may occur (reorganization of belief structure). Once a favorable attitude toward purchase of the brand occurs, changes in the conative component (intentions to behave, trial, etc.) will occur (see Figure 6-3). Ray refers to this sequence as the "learn-feel-do" hierarchy.[40]

As Ray indicates, the learning hierarchy exists only in special circumstances. It is most likely to occur in situations in which there are audience involvement, product differentiation, and emphasis on the mass media in communication, and where the product is in the early stages of the product life cycle.[41] Product examples include portable television sets, autos, washing machines, and pocket calculators.[42]

THE DISSONANCE-ATTRIBUTION HIERARCHY. Another view of the organization of the cognitive, affective, conative structure is called the dissonance-attribution hierarchy. This is the exact reverse of the learning hierarchy—"do-feel-learn" instead of "learn-feel-do"; in the dissonance-attribution hierarchy behavior occurs first, then attitude change, and finally learning[43] (see Figure 6-4).

FIGURE 6-3
The Learning Hierarchy

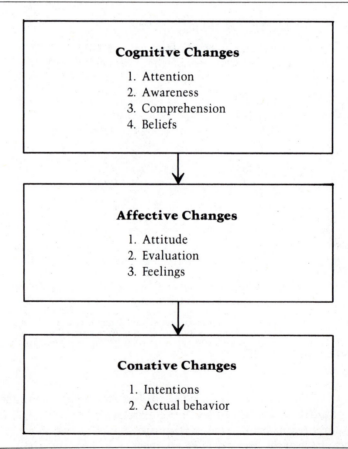

FIGURE 6-4
The Dissonance-Attribution Hierarchy

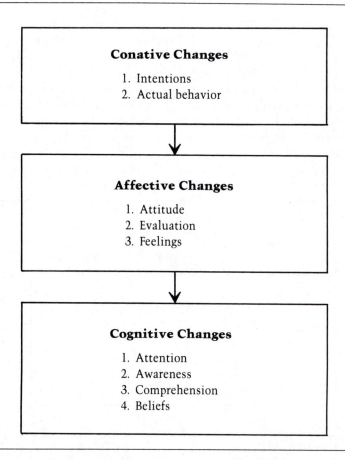

Although studies in dissonance theory have been applied to this model, Ray indicates that attribution theory may be a more up-to-date explanation of this hierarchy. The reasoning for this approach would be as follows: The basic idea is that people determine that they have attitudes by perceiving their own behavior. If someone has made a brand choice, this person will say, "I must have a positive attitude toward that brand because I have chosen it." If, after choice and attitude change, individuals are exposed to marketing messages, they will tend to choose the information that will support their attitude. Product examples might be autos and home entertainment equipment.[44]

The dissonance-attribution hierarchy has been found to occur when the following conditions exist:

1. Low differentiation for complex alternatives
2. Non-mass media, personal sources important

3. Mature stage in the product life cycle
4. Involving situation[45]

   THE LOW-INVOLVEMENT HIERARCHY. A third approach is called the low-involvement hierarchy, or "learn-do-feel"[46] (see Figure 6-5). The low-involvement hierarchy views information as first changing the cognitive component, then bringing about actual behavior changes, and then finally affecting attitude. The view holds that television viewers, for example, are not involved with the advertising. Thus, there is little perceptual defense against the commercial messages. Although television commercials will probably not change attitudes, they may, after a great deal of repetition, make possible a shift in cognitive structure. Consumers will thus be better able to recall the name of a product or service that has been advertised. The next time they are in a store, that name could come to mind and result in a purchase. After the consumer has

FIGURE 6-5
The Low-Involvement Hierarchy

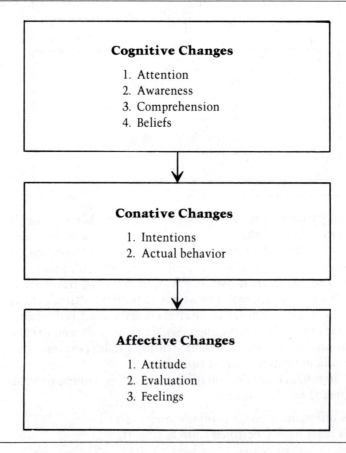

used the product, it is contended, attitude shift will occur. If product usage is satisfactory, a more favorable attitude toward the product will develop; if usage is unsatisfactory, a negative attitude will develop. Examples of products that often fit this profile are soaps, mouthwashes, and gum—often heavily advertised products.

Low involvement is likely to occur under the following conditions:[47]

1. Low differentiation
2. Mass media important
3. Mature stage in the product life cycle

THE BATRA-RAY MODEL. Batra and Ray have moved beyond these three basic models to develop a fourth approach.[48] Their model would appear as shown in Figure 6-6. Batra and Ray argue that attitude change can stem from two different sources of affect, affect developed on the

FIGURE 6-6
The Batra-Ray Model

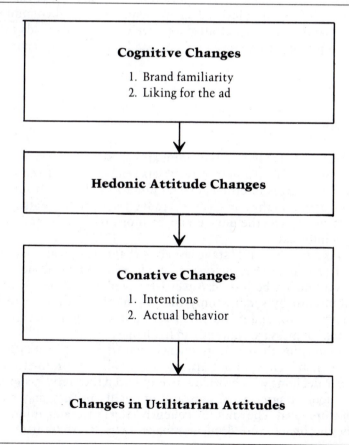

Cognitive Changes

1. Brand familiarity
2. Liking for the ad

Hedonic Attitude Changes

Conative Changes

1. Intentions
2. Actual behavior

Changes in Utilitarian Attitudes

basis of cognitive appraisal of the brand and affect based on the advertisement itself. The latter affect arises from the presentation of "complex messages, combining vignettes, role portrayals, attractive (or unattractive visuals), and the like. Some of these elements persuade, others evoke technical appreciation, some irritate, others create a need of 'upbeat' surging while others create moods that are heartwarming, or just plain relaxing or soothing."[49] In other words, this component could be viewed as ad execution likability.

Batra and Ray have argued that in low-involvement situations the key attitudinal component is advertising execution—based on the hedonic component. For more high-involvement situations the attribute-based utilitarian attitude component would be more important. A key point is that affect is not absent (prior to purchase intention, behavior) from the low-involvement hierarchy.

If further studies prove Batra and Ray to be correct, it is clear that advertising works not only by presenting cognitive information to the consumer but also by developing feelings, moods, or emotions. In a marketplace of parity products, this "emotion strategy" may prove that those supposedly "information-less" advertisements are indeed communicating to the consumer. This strategy of developing "likable" ads may be most appropriate for the reinforcement and reminder mechanisms of Sheth.

SUMMARY

We have attempted to look at the information system in the marketplace via advertisers and consumers. Advertisers send messages to consumers with varying degrees of efficiency and professionalism. Consumers in turn receive some of the messages from advertisers, but they also look to their own memories, the advice and opinions of friends, and neutral sources of information.

If we take an "objective" stance, such as that of classical economists, we would have to say that the system of information flow in the marketplace leaves much to be desired. Advertisers, predictably, operate in their own self-interest by sending only the information they wish to send, when they wish to send it, and often with uncertain guidance as to the proper "mix" of message content and frequency.

Consumers, for their part, frequently fail to meet the standards of "economic man." They do not always collect all the information they could when deciding which product to buy. Often they rely on shortcuts; they may look to price as an indicator of quality or they may become brand or store loyal. They not infrequently stop processing information when they become confused and may make "snap" decisions just to "get it over with."

But from another vantage point, the market of information flow tends to operate in a generally acceptable manner. If we accept our existing economic system, it is perfectly logical for advertisers to operate in their own self-interest by transmitting persuasive communications which are repeated often. They are attempting to induce sales to ensure the continued existence of the firm.

Although consumers do not always try to find perfect solutions to their purchase decisions, they operate in ways that often lead to subjective satisfaction on their part. Consumers will often informally balance the cost of seeking additional information with the benefits they hope it will bring to the final purchase decision. If it appears that additional information is not needed, they will not collect it. This does not necessarily mean that they are not "rational," but only that they are operating from a set of decision-making rules that they have found acceptable in making purchases. If consumers attempted to behave in the rational manner that classical economists have posited, they probably would spend a great deal of their time gathering information. Consumers are constantly seeking products and services that will allow them more leisure time. It is not different with information seeking. Consumers are always seeking ways to reduce search time, yet still reach acceptable decisions.

This is not to say that consumers do not buy products that are unacceptable for their existing needs. When this happens, it is very difficult to determine whether it is the fault of the "imperfect" market sources or the fault of the "imperfect" consumer. If you make a mistake in a purchase decision, it may be easier to blame (say) the advertising system than to accept the blame yourself.

Advertising can be seen to be involved in a market service. It provides a type of information that helps match buyers and sellers in a general system emphasizing the self-interest of the participants. It is clearly not "perfect," and could certainly be improved. But any steps toward improvement must rest on an understanding of the ways consumers actually utilize information.

More and more information is apparently not the answer. Consumers will continue to use shortcuts in their purchasing behavior. What is apparently needed is not more, but better, information. Unfortunately, neither critics nor supporters of advertising are exactly sure what "better" information is. There is little prospect that we can make the consumer the perfect information procuring and processing system. All we can hope for is to make the consumer a better information system, given the "recalcitrance and perversity" of human nature.

Advertising can be constantly improved in terms of information output, but that is only one side of the issue. The consumer must also be improved through better consumer education, learning not only how to obtain information but how to use it. Most of all, the consumer must *want* to use the information.

Notes

1. Jagdish N. Sheth, "Measurement of Advertising Effectiveness: Some Theoretical Considerations," *Journal of Advertising,* vol. 3, no. 1 (1974), pp. 8-11.
2. Neil H. Borden, *The Economic Effect of Advertising* (Chicago: Irwin, 1942).
3. Raymond L. Horton, *Buyer Behavior: A Decision-Making Approach* (Columbus, Ohio: Charles E. Merrill Publishing Co., 1984), p. 12.
4. See Jacob Jacoby, Donald E. Speller, and Carol A. Kohn, "Brand Choice Behavior as a Function of Information Load," *Journal of Marketing Research,* 11 (February, 1984), pp. 63-69; William L. Wilkie, "Analysis of Effects of Information Load," *Journal of Marketing Research* 11 (November, 1974), pp. 462-466; John O. Summers, "Less Information Is Better?," *Journal of Marketing Research* 11 (November, 1974), pp. 467-468; and Gerald Zaltman and Melanie Wallendorf, *Consumer Behavior: Basic Findings and Management Implications 2/E* (New York: John Wiley & Sons, Inc., 1983), pp. 351-353.
5. James A. March and Herbert A. Simon, *Organizations* (New York: John Wiley & Sons, Inc., 1958), pp. 203-204.
6. Raymond A. Bauer, "Consumer Behavior as Risk Taking," in *Dynamic Marketing for a Changing World,* ed. Robert S. Hancock (Chicago: American Marketing Association, 1960), pp. 389, 398.
7. Del I. Hawkins, Roger J. Best, and Kenneth A. Coney, *Consumer Behavior: Implications for Marketing Strategy* (Plano, Tex.: Business Publications, Inc., 1983), p. 483.
8. E. C. Hirschman and M. K. Mills, "Sources Shoppers Use to Pick Stores," *Journal of Advertising Research,* February, 1980, pp. 47-51.
9. Carol A. Kohn Berning and Jacob Jacoby, "Patterns of Information Acquisition in New Product Purchases," *Journal of Consumer Research,* 1 (September, 1974), pp. 8-12, and George Kotona and Eva Mueller, "A Study of Purchase Decisions," in *Consumer Behavior: The Dynamics of Consumer Reactions,* ed. L. H. Clark (New York: New York University Press, 1955), pp. 35-87.
10. Horton, op. cit., p. 271.
11. Ibid.
12. Robert B. Settle, "Attribution Theory and Acceptance of Information," *Journal of Marketing Research,* 9 (February, 1972), pp. 85-88.
13. Thomas S. Robertson, "The Effect of the Informal Group Upon Member Innovative Behavior," in *Marketing and the New Science of Planning,* ed. Robert L. King (Chicago: American Marketing Association, 1968), pp. 334-340.
14. Ben M. Enis and Gordon W. Paul, "Store Loyalty as a Basis for Market Segmentation," *Journal of Retailing,* 46 (Fall, 1970), p. 46.

15. Bauer, op. cit., p. 87.
16. Leon G. Schiffman and Leslie Lazar Kanuk, *Consumer Behavior* (Englewood Cliffs, N.J.: Prentice-Hall, 1983), p. 160.
17. Donald F. Cox, *Risk Taking and Information Handling in Consumer Behavior,* ed. Donald F. Cox (Boston: Division of Research, Graduate School of Business Administration, Harvard University, 1967).
18. Schiffman and Kanuk, op. cit., p. 161.
19. Ibid., p. 163.
20. Ted Roselius, "Consumer Ranking of Risk Reduction Methods, *Journal of Marketing,* 35 (January, 1971), p. 61.
21. Cox, op. cit., p. 9.
22. M. Venkatesan, "Cognitive Consistency and Novelty Seeking," *Consumer Behavior: Theoretical Sources,* ed. Scott Ward and Thomas S. Robertson (Englewood Cliffs, N.J.: Prentice-Hall, 1973), pp. 355-384.
23. John D. Claxton, Joseph N. Fry, and Bernard Portis, "A Taxonomy of Prepurchase Information Gathering Patterns," *Journal of Consumer Research,* 1 (December, 1974), pp. 35-42.
24. Jacob Jacoby, Robert W. Chestnut, and William A. Fisher, "A Behaviorial Process Approach to Information Acquisition in Nondurable Purchasing," *Journal of Marketing Research,* 15 (November, 1978), pp. 532-544.
25. William L. Moore and Donald R. Lehmann, "Individual Differences in Search Behavior for a Nondurable Product," *Journal of Consumer Research,* 7 (December, 1980), pp. 296-307.
26. Ibid.
27. Peter D. Bennett and Robert M. Mandel, "Prepurchase Information-seeking Behavior of New Car Purchases—The Learning Hypothesis," *Journal of Marketing Research,* 6 (November, 1969), pp. 430-433.
28. William P. Dommermuth, "The Shopping Matrix and Marketing Strategy," *Journal of Marketing Research,* 2 (1965), pp. 128-132.
29. Hawkins et al., op. cit., pp. 418-432.
30. Ham B. Thorelli, Helmut Becher, and Jack Engledow, *The Information Seekers* (Cambridge, Mass.: Bellinger Publishing Co., 1975).
31. James R. Bettman, *An Information Processing Theory of Consumer Choice* (Reading, Mass.: Addison-Wesley, 1979), ch. 5.
32. Joseph W. Newman, "Consumer External Search: Amount and Determinants," in *Consumer and Industrial Buying Behavior,* ed. A. G. Woodside, J. N. Sheth, and P. D. Bennett (New York: North Holland Publishing Co., 1977), pp. 79-94.
33. Hawkins et al., op. cit., p. 530.
34. Ibid., p. 528.
35. Ibid., p. 526.
36. Ibid., p. 530.

37. Schiffman and Kanuk, op. cit., p. 546.

38. S. M. Shugan, "The Cost of Thinking," *Journal of Consumer Research*, September, 1980, pp. 99-111.

39. N. K. Malhotra, "Multi-stage Information Processing Behavior," *Journal of the Academy of Marketing Science*, Winter, 1982, pp. 54-71.

40. Michael L. Ray, *Advertising and Communication Management* (Englewood Cliffs, N.J.: Prentice-Hall, 1982), pp. 184-185.

41. Ibid.

42. Michael L. Ray, "Marketing Communications and the Hierarchy-of-Effects," in *New Models for Mass Communication*, ed. Peter Clarke (Beverly Hills, Calif.: Sage Publications, Inc., 1973), p. 152.

43. Ray, *Advertising and Communication Management*, pp. 185-186.

44. Ibid., p. 186.

45. Ibid., p. 187.

46. Ibid.

47. Ibid.

48. R. Batra and Michael L. Ray, "How Advertising Works at Contact," Working Paper (Stanford University School of Business Administration, 1983).

49. Ibid., p. 5.

Chapter 7

Advertising and the Media

In this chapter we will discuss the media as social institutions, the functions society expects them to perform, and their relationship to advertising. Our discussion will pertain primarily to television, radio, newspapers, and magazines. Given this perspective, the reader should not expect this chapter to deal with the more functional media material, such as factors in media selection, reach, frequency, media exposure models, and the differences between the various media vehicles.

Nor will we concentrate on issues such as the alleged bias towards the interest of advertisers in editorial content, or the economic implications of the advertising "subsidy." These are covered elsewhere, and the curious reader is encouraged to pursue more specialized sources.[1]

Instead we will focus on the advertising message as a part of the larger media institutional directive of serving as a forum for learning and debating the character of our culture. It is an area of advertising's evolution in this country that has received particular attention in the last 15 years,[2] and is, we feel, deserving of particular analysis here.

MEDIA-GOVERNMENT RELATIONSHIPS

Two basic theories of media-government relationships are generally recognized. The *authoritarian theory* is the older of the two. Its origin is associated with the era of authoritarian governments. Under this theory the media are, in essence, controlled by government and are used to inform people of what the authorities want them to know. Furthermore, the government functions as a gatekeeper to keep out of the media any information that it feels might be detrimental to its authority. The media are thus servants of the state. This theory is still held by most totalitarian governments and is at times embraced by democratic regimes when the position of the party in power is endangered.

The *libertarian theory* (i.e., based on classical liberalism) characterizes the manner in which the media presumably function in a democratic society. Although libertarian writings refer mainly to "the press," Siebert's summary of the theory can be readily extended to pertain to all the media:

> The press is not an instrument of government, but rather a device for presenting evidence and arguments on the basis of which the people can check on government and make up their minds as to policy. Therefore, it is imperative that the press be free from government control and influence. In order for truth to emerge, all ideas must get a fair hearing; there must be a "free market place" of ideas and information. Minorities as well as the strong must have access to the press. This is the theory of the press that was written into our Bill of Rights.[3]

Under the libertarian theory, the free press (media) is expected to perform certain functions for the benefit of society. Theodore Peterson has detailed these functions as follows:

> (1) servicing the political system by providing information, discussion, and debate on public affairs; (2) enlightening the public so as to make it capable of self-government; (3) safeguarding the rights of the individual by serving as a watchdog against government; (4) servicing the economic system, primarily by bringing together the buyers and sellers of goods and services through the medium of advertising; (5) providing entertainment; (6) maintaining its own financial self-sufficiency so as to be free from the pressures of special interests.[4]

No specific mention of freedom of speech is included in the functions listed above. This may seem strange in light of the fact that freedom of speech and freedom of the press (media) have been, almost universally, linked together. Scholars have generally held that the reason for constitutional guarantees of freedom of the press was that the press provided the basic machinery for transmitting information and ideas to the people. However, there would be little value in upholding the freedom to speak if the instruments for distributing speech could be curtailed or controlled.

THE MEDIA AS DISTRIBUTORS OF "SPEECH"

Members of the media have generally conceived freedom of speech to be freedom for the media to speak as they wish without fear of government restraints or penalty. Such freedom would then prohibit government from acting as a gatekeeper to open or close the gate at its will in respect to what news, ideas, and concepts should be passed on to the people.

But even then it is idealistic to expect the media to speak for (or to) all citizens. Given this perspective, it can be contended there must also be freedom for the lay citizen to speak—to lay what sentiments he or she pleases before the public. Perhaps society, then, should expect the media not only to be free to speak as they wish but also to serve as distributors of speech by lay citizens who wish to reach large numbers of people. In light of this concept, a seventh function of the media may be suggested as an addition to the six functions given by Peterson—providing facilities for distribution of messages by citizens and making such facilities available without discrimination.

A consideration of various aspects of this seventh function—why it is important and how it might be implemented—is in order. If people are to be kept informed, not only of current news but also of divergent ideas, it is essential that the anti-establishment person, the muckraker, the protester, and the "crackpot," as well as "members of the club," have access to the eyes and ears of the public.

Is this not possible now? Arguably it is not, because of (a) media concentration, (b) the media as gatekeepers, and (c) diversity. *Is* concentration (i.e., inadequate representativeness) a problem? Let us turn to some hard data dealing with the issue. We will review data for newspapers, magazines, television, and radio.

Media Concentration

There are 1,730 daily newspapers in the United States with a total daily circulation of approximately 61 million readers. Twenty newspaper companies control more than half the daily sales. One percent of the owners own approximately 34 percent of all papers sold daily. In 1900 there were 2,042 daily newspapers and 2,023 owners. By 1980, there were 1,730 dailies and 760 owners. In 1900 there was an average of one newspaper owner for each 38,000 citizens, while in 1980 the average newspaper owner provided news for 300,000 consumers.[5]

There are many other types of newspapers, such as weeklies, biweeklies, triweeklies, and free-circulation papers. Although their presence surely weakens the concentration figures cited above for dailies, their ability to disseminate information and their impact in a meaningful "marketplace of ideas" is problematic.

There are approximately 10,830 magazines. Based on a measure of the proportion of sales controlled by each owner, twenty corporations earn just over 50 percent of the total annual industry revenues of $12 billion.[6]

The three major networks, ABC, CBS, and NBC, together with their owned and operated television stations in major markets, received more than half of the $8.8 billion of television revenues in 1980.[7] Will these concentration figures for television decrease in the future as the penetration of cable television systems continues? It is a difficult question. Since many of these systems are being purchased by the existing networks, it is possible that these concentration numbers will actually increase.

Radio stations follow the same profile. Of the over 8,000 commercially operated radio stations, ten corporations have well over half the audience for AM and FM commercial radio.[8]

Reviewing this quantitative data, it appears that concentration of media ownership is strong. How does this affect the quality of the media?

Eversole found that newspapers that were once competitive but were made monopolies by chains produced "higher prices and lower quality."[9] The Brookings Institution, on the other hand, showed that though chain-owned papers charge 7 percent more for ads than independent papers, chains operating in areas where there are competitive papers have advertising rates 15 percent lower than those for their other chain-owned papers.[10] Keller found that serious news content was 23 percent less in chain-owned than in independent papers,[11] while Thrift found that 85 percent of chain papers publish uniform political endorsements.[12]

Are the media being adversely affected by the increase in media concentration? There would appear to be cause for concern.

The Media as Gatekeepers

In many respects, the media function as gatekeepers. Recent court decisions have interpreted freedom of the press to mean freedom to publish or broadcast, therefore solidifying the idea that publishers and broadcasters make the ultimate decisions concerning what should and should not go into or on their newspapers or magazines, radio stations or television stations. This certainly includes advertising space and air time. The basic premise that the media use in rejecting news or advertising materials is the "best interest" concept. Presumably, materials that are not in the "best interest" of the particular media vehicle or the public it serves should not be utilized. The problem is whether media management is in a position to (or should) judge what is in the best interest of the public.

What is interesting is that the courts have generally placed many restrictions on the government concerning actions it might take to influence news or editorial content as well as the advertising placed in the media. Both areas have been granted some First Amendment protection. In its purest form this principle is expressed in the statement that "above all else, the First Amendment means that government has no power to restrict expression because of its message, its ideas, its subject matter, or its content."[13]

Although advertising or commercial speech has more limited First

Amendment protection than news or editorial material,[14,15] it seems ironic that advertising messages protected from government interference can subsequently not appear because the media decides they should not.

Have the media utilized their gatekeeping function? Some newspapers have refused to accept advertisements by gay activists; others have refused stories that might offend or threaten the business interests of the directors of the newspaper. *The Baltimore Sun* killed a story describing imminent labor negotiations between hospital workers and the management of Johns Hopkins Hospital in Baltimore. Apparently a director of the *Sun* was a director of Johns Hopkins Hospital and also a director of the Mercantile Safe Deposit & Trust Company, which held 61.3 percent of the shares in the newspaper company.[16] Many countercommercials (messages developed by citizen groups to respond to television commercials dealing with controversial subjects such as health, nutrition, medical claims, etc.) were refused access to the media in the 1970's.

The Key Question of Diversity

It may be contended that the central issue in the dissemination of ideas and information in the libertarian or neo-liberal media environment is that of diversity. The essence of diversity is that as many voices as possible must be represented. Within this general framework, two schools of thought can be isolated.

The first is skeptical of any regulation, and assumes that the free and open marketplace is the best possible environment in which diversity can flourish. The premise of this position is that a fluid, competitive marketplace will permit all sectors of the population to enter the system and provide needed information-communication services. The real problem is how to provide profit incentives to attract the risk capital that will be needed to accomplish the goal of additional information-communication services. The key measurement criterion to judge success would be quantity of channels. This school believes that if there is a sufficient quantity of channels, and the freedom to open new ones, an acceptable level of diversity can be achieved.[17]

The second school argues:

 that in this era of giant national and transnational corporate dominance it is absurd to presuppose that there is sufficient equitable distribution of economic power to allow market forces alone to assume equitable distribution of services. The political decision-making process is so manipulated by powerful corporations that it is virtually impossible for citizens' groups, consumers, minorities and the power sector of society to participate significantly in the policy-making process. Access to information is such a basic human right and communication so central in the development of national cultures that these should be considered a common good and a public trust. Information should not be considered simply a marketplace commodity distributed only to those with capacity to pay.

For this group the starting point of research on economic concentration should be the problem area of content bias: images of women and minorities, the presence of poverty and other injustices.[18]

The question here, then, is how the economically and socially less powerful can be given access to the media. For this school of thought, what is important is not the *quantity* of channels but their *quality* .

Thus there are clearly philosophical differences on how to achieve diversity. But another way to examine this issue is to pose the essential question: diversity for what? Diversity, it may be argued, so that different views are expressed. But to whom should these views be expressed? Only the believers? And, if so, to what end?

Putting it another way, if we have quantitative diversity, there will logically be many different media vehicles available for the expression of differing views. But, if media vehicles are increasingly specialized by interest groups, the views that are likely to be expressed will tend to be comforting rather than controversial, placid rather than provoking. We choose media vehicles to reflect our own relatively narrow interests, and the content reflects these biases.

Thus a case may be made that in order to achieve true diversity in the sense of individuals being confronted with challenging (new, provocative, unfamiliar) points of view, access needs to be gained in a qualitative sense. In short, rather than striving for *more* media vehicles, the aims of diversity might best be served by attempting to enrich the "marketplace of ideas" *within* the existing media structure. And that, of course, requires a fresh look at the media as gatekeepers.

THE MEDIA AS "COMMON CARRIERS"

To set the stage for the following discussion, consider the following proposition:

> The services and facilities provided by the media are so vital to the functioning of a political democracy and economy based on a "free" market system that access to it must be made available to all who would use its facilities. This proposition is so fundamental that society should expect the media to operate within a framework comparable to that associated with transportation common carriers.

If one accepts the concept that media should not be permitted to function as gatekeepers, in ways that thwart a truly diverse marketplace of ideas, then it naturally follows that there should be freedom of access to the media on some reasonable basis. How can this be accomplished? One perspective is that the mass media should operate as common carriers with respect to the advertising space and time offered to the public.

Assume that owners of the mass media operate two distinct enterprises. One consists of providing the public with news, entertainment, analysis, and personal views through editorial material. The other consists of selling advertising space or time to those who wish to buy it for purposes of presenting their own messages to readers/listeners/viewers. This latter enterprise the media call advertising.

In many respects it can be argued that the media operate a transportation facility. They provide the organization, equipment, and facilities for loading on communication material of their own choosing, then transport and deliver it to specific destinations. In addition to the space or time needed to carry their own material, they provide empty space which they rent to others.

It is this rentable dimension that might well be treated as a service offered by a common carrier. In transporting their own communications material the media can be seen as operating as private carriers. They may purchase the Doonesbury cartoon or the Independent News and transport this material to their readers/listeners/viewers, but that type of material is used to further their own news-editorial-entertainment function. Transportation facilities needed to distribute such material become an organic part of the media operation and, by this reasoning, need not be considered part of the service of a common carrier.

The media's "rentable" units are another matter. That space is offered to the public at large. It provides the most viable facility for businesses or citizens to reach mass audiences with commercial or personal messages. Arguably, it is important in a political and economic democracy to expect the mass media to provide such facilities without discrimination. The application of the common carrier concept should accomplish that.

Responsibilities of Common Carriers

It is the duty of a common carrier to make its facilities available without discrimination. This is a key element and curtails some of the power usually associated with private ownership. The facility is considered so important to so many segments of society that this, in itself, sets it somewhat apart from most private enterprises. It is, in fact, clothed with public interest.

Any review of the history of railway transportation in the United States will reveal the logic of giving it common carrier status. Before such status was legally established, railroads literally exercised economic life-or-death power over individual shippers. No producer of raw materials or manufactured goods could long survive if denied access to transportation facilities or forced to pay more than the competition for such facilities.

A historic case in preregulatory days is that of Standard Oil. John D. Rockefeller, Sr., arranged a deal which, in essence, provided that he would ship all his company's oil via railroad A, in return for which A would either refuse to carry the oil of Standard's competitors or charge them substantially more than Standard paid. Few, if any, competitors could survive under such a handicap. The widespread practice of discrimination in both price and service led to the passage of the Interstate Commerce Act in 1887.

A good case could be made in support of the proposition that advertising is so important to the economic health of producers and vendors of goods and services that discrimination by media in the form of refusal of access or in prices could bring prosperity to one firm and failure to another. Indeed, there has been little evidence of media discrimination among advertisers of goods and services. Of course, some media have refused to sell advertising time or space to any product falling within a particular classification—for example, tobacco, hard liquor, or X-rated movies. Such refusal does not, however, violate the common carrier principle. A railroad can legitimately choose not to accept high explosives for shipment so long as such refusal applies to all would-be shippers of such commodities.

However, there have been instances of media discrimination among advertisers of products or services that fall in the same classification. Thus, some media have tried to protect local dealers of automobiles or appliances by refusing the advertising of dealers in neighboring towns. In the early days of the chain store, publishers often refused advertising from chains while accepting advertising from independents. Such practices were often the result of pressure by established businesses that feared the competition of new firms. When discount record houses were getting started, some failed because they were not allowed to use local advertising media. The media were intimidated by traditional record shops, which threatened to stop their purchase of space or time if the media accepted advertising from the new discount entrants into the field. Such pressure would be largely eliminated if the common carrier concept were applied to the advertising segment of the media.

The media that practice discrimination are, in fact, gatekeepers. They effectively deny the innovator and competitor freedom to speak to the public and, also, effectively deny the right of the public to know what is new and different or more economical. Furthermore, they can increase the profitability of one enterprise and cause the failure of another.

Application to Noncommercial Messages

While advertising has been used primarily to promote the sale of material goods and services, it is by no means confined to that. It can be made equally available to those who wish to inform and persuade people with respect to a city bond issue, the need for better educational facilities, the merits of a particular political candidate, approaches to meeting the problems of pollution in modern society, alternative sexual preferences, positions on abortion or busing, or any other sentiment held by any individual or group that wishes to present such sentiment to the public.

In short, from the perspective established earlier in this chapter, the institution of advertising can be used to make the freedom to speak vastly more available than has been true in the past. Through the use of advertising the lay citizen can become her or his own editor. The purchase of newspaper space or a segment of broadcast time can give the individual the right to present his or her own message, in his or her own words, and without the fear of having this message edited or cut by the seller of space or time. Such advertising is often referred to as an "advertorial." Of course, the publisher can establish certain standards on how the message is to be "packaged" (e.g., no obscenity), but otherwise there should presumably be no interference.

The renter of space is given essentially the same freedom as that possessed by the editor of the paper. In essence the individual becomes a part of the press and thus enjoys the freedom the press has long enjoyed. This concept was established by the landmark U.S. Supreme Court Case, *New York Times Co. vs. Sullivan* (March 10, 1964).[19]

What was the background of that case? In 1960 a group of serious citizens wanted to get a message before a large audience to point up the problems of blacks in the South. They chose a large advertisement in *The New York Times* as a method of doing so. Among other things, the message criticized public officials. That criticism brought violent reaction from some officials who sued the *Times* and the advertisers for libel. The plaintiff argued that because the message appeared as a paid advertisement it did not have the protection of the First Amendment.

The court decision denied the plaintiff's claim. It held that "any other conclusion would discourage newspapers from carrying 'editorial advertisements' [i.e., "advertorials"] of this type, and so might shut off an important outlet for the promulgation of information and ideas by persons who do not themselves have access to publishing facilities—who wish to exercise their freedom of speech even though they are not members of the press."[20]

It should be noted, however, that while this case significantly strengthened the position of those interested in communicating through advertorial materials, it still did not place any restriction on the media's right to reject an advertorial if it is judged to be not in the best interest of the media vehicle or the public it serves.

Broadcasters in particular have been very reluctant to accept any advertising that appears controversial, lest they be required under any interpretation of the fairness doctrine to provide equal time for presentation of an opposing view. The print media, unfettered by any fairness concept, have continued to accept or not accept advertising on controversial subjects as standards dictate.

SUMMARY

The provision, by the media, of facilities for the distribution of messages by citizens and making such facilities available without discrimination was a key point in this chapter. The issues of concentration and media diversity were discussed as possible impediments to the provision of this function. It was also made clear that the media can act as gatekeepers for many of the issues that concerned citizens would like to transmit. Given the facts of concentration, diversity, and gatekeeping, a proposal was made to reconstruct the current view of the media into that of common carriers, facilities for the transportation of ideas. These "facilities" would accept controversial ideas from the public without discrimination in the "rentable" portion of their business.

Notes

1. For further information see Vincent P. Norris, "Consumer Magazine Prices and the Mythical Advertising Subsidy," *Journalism Quarterly* 59:2 (Summer, 1982), and R. C. Smith. "The Magazines' Smoking Habit," *Columbia Journalism Review*, January/February, 1978.
2. For a more in-depth discussion, the reader is referred to Charles H. Sandage, Vernon Fryburger, and Kim Rotzoll, *Advertising Theory and Practice* (Homewood, Ill.: Richard D. Irwin, Inc., 1983), pp. 81-92.
3. Frederick Siebert, in *Four Theories of the Press*, ed. Frederick Siebert, Theodore Peterson, and Wilbur Schramm (Urbana: University of Illinois Press, 1956), pp. 3-4.
4. Theodore Peterson, in ibid., p. 74.
5. Ben H. Bagdikian, *The Media Monopoly* (Boston, Mass.: Beacon Press, 1983), pp. 8-9.
6. Ibid., p. 14.
7. Ibid.
8. Ibid., pp. 14, 15.
9. Pam Eversole, "Consolidation of Newspapers: What Happens to the Consumer?," *Journalism Quarterly*, Summer, 1971, p. 245.
10. *Straus Editors' Report*, December 13, 1969, p. 1.
11. Kristine Keller, "Quantity of New in Group-Owned and Independent Papers: Independent Papers Have More," Master's Thesis, Graduate School of Journalism, University of California, Berkeley, 1978.
12. Ralph R. Thrift, Jr., "How Chain Ownership Affects Editorial Vigor of Newspapers," *Journalism Quarterly*, Summer, 1967, p. 329.

13. *Police Dept of Chicago* vs *Mosley,* 408 U.S. 92, 96 (1971).
14. *Virginia State Board of Pharmacy* vs. *Virginia Citizens Consumer Council,* 425 U.S. 748 (1976).
15. *Central Hudson Gas & Electric Corp.* vs. *Public Service Comm'n,* 433 U.S. 350 (1977).
16. Bagdikian, op. cit., pp. 3-4.
17. Robert A. White, "What Kind of Media Diversity?," *Communication Research Trends* (London: Centre for the Study of Communication and Culture, 1983), vol. 4, no. 1, p. 7.
18. Ibid., p. 7.
19. *New York Times Co.* vs. *Sullivan,* 376 U.S. 254 (1964).
20. Ibid.

Chapter 8

Advertising and Regulation

This chapter will deal with the question, What forces should be allowed to regulate the institution of advertising? Should it be regulated by natural market forces, organized market forces (consumerism), self-regulatory forces, governmental forces, or media forces? (see Figure 8-1). Are these mutually exclusive approaches or synergistic when operating simultaneously?

NATURAL MARKET FORCES

As discussed in Chapter 2, the market is presumed, in the best of worlds, to be entirely self-regulating. Consumers will always seek out the lowest prices for products or services. If consumers find some advertising to be inadequate, they will turn away from it and seek other competitive advertising sources that will satisfy their information needs.

Advertisers will promote their products or services in their own self-interest, and this advertising will be successful only if it is in agreement with the self-interest of potential buyers. If advertisers find their messages are deficient in this regard, they will alter their practices or lose their competitive advantage.

It is the simple yet complex world of Adam Smith. There may be some short-term aberrations, but in the long run the market will make appropriate adjustments, if allowed to run its own course. Or could it be that the long run does not matter, as significant damage could be done in the short run?

FIGURE 8-1
The Forces of Regulation

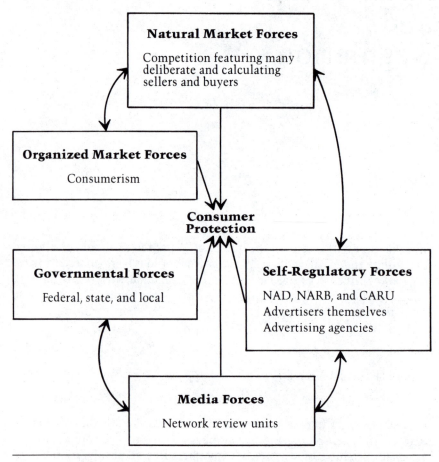

Source: Adapted from Jagdish N. Sheth and Nicholas Mammana, "Why Consumer Protection Efforts Are Likely to Fail," Faculty Working Paper, No. 104 (Urbana-Champaign: University of Illinois, College of Commerce and Business Administration, April 11, 1985).

ORGANIZED MARKET FORCES (CONSUMERISM)

"Consumerism" is a word that can be defined in many different ways. Betty Furness has described it as follows: "Consumerism is an effort to put the buyer on an equal footing with the seller. Consumers want to know what they're buying. What they're eating. How long a product will last. What it will and will not do. Whether it will be safe for them and/or the environment."[1]

A somewhat broader view is offered by Aaker: "Consumerism is an evolving set of activities of government, business, independent organizations, and concerned consumers that are designed to protect the rights of consumers. It is an evolving, dynamic movement with an enlarging scope and changing spokesmen and issues. It is action oriented and, therefore, more than an analysis of problems."[2]

History of the Consumer Movement

Is consumerism a new idea? Certainly not. Consumers were attempting to cooperate in a number of ways to improve their situation as early as 1844. For it was in this year that poor weavers in Rochdale, England, formed the first "co-op" of consumers.[3]

Although many groups and individuals were active in consumer issues during the late 1800s in this country, it was not until Upton Sinclair's *The Jungle*[4] that consumerists were generally able to see tangible results for their efforts. This book, along with articles in the *Ladies Home Journal, Collier's Weekly*, and *Good Housekeeping* concerning patent-medicine abuses, ushered in the era of the "muckrakers," writers who investigated and publicized alleged corruption and improper practices in industry and government.[5]

Sinclair's book dealt with the unsanitary conditions and fraud that existed in the meat-packing industry. This powerful exposé, combined with the leadership of Dr. Harvey W. Wiley, Chief of the Bureau of Chemistry in the Department of Agriculture, helped lead to the passage of the Pure Food and Drug Act of 1906, which made it unlawful to transmit between states adulterated or misbranded food or drugs. This law was a landmark in that it represented the first major shift in the attitude of the federal government from a philosophy of *caveat emptor* (Let the buyer beware) to one of *caveat venditor* (Let the seller beware).[6]

Advertising, of course, received its share of attention during the muckrakers' period. In the early 1900s, *Printer's Ink* magazine established a set of legal standards to help eliminate misleading and deceptive advertising. Many consumerists lobbied for this model statute, and it subsequently became law in many states. A far more important piece of legislation which dealt with advertising was passed by Congress in 1914. Although the Federal Trade Commission Act was established primarily to deal with antitrust matters and unfair methods of competition, the newly formed commission quickly interpreted the act as a weapon against deceptive interstate advertising practices.[7]

Certainly this is not a complete picture of what happened during this tumultuous era. It can be said, however, that for the first time large numbers of consumers were made aware of the potentially dangerous consequences of consumption. The edifice of the market had begun to show signs of strain.

The thrust of the consumer movement was reduced by the period of affluence that followed in the 1920s. Many of the heated issues were set aside or forgotten, and many of the existing laws were not adequately enforced, owing in part to key court decisions. In *FTC* vs. *Raladam Co.*,[8] for example, the court held that the Federal Trade Commission must find that not only consumers but also competitors were injured by the misrepresentation. This was a situation (the competitor's injury) which was extremely difficult to prove in court.

With publication of *Your Money's Worth* by Stuart Chase and Frederick J. Schlink in 1927, the "movement" again came alive. The book became a bestseller because of such comments as: Bar soap for women is made with "a little creosol, a common and cheap disinfectant recommended by the government for disinfecting cars, barns, and chicken yards."[9] Over the next decade this book seemed to spawn a series of others that criticized advertising and indicated that the consumer was being deceived. They included *Skin Deep*[10] and *Eat, Drink, and Be Wary.*[11]

Of the attacks made on advertising, many were bitter and far-reaching. These challenges were different from previous ones in that critics struck at the very existence of advertising rather than merely its excesses or the products that advertising promoted.

Thus the spotlight turned once again to the imperfect marketplace. Spurred by the devastating effects of the Great Depression, consumers and governmental bodies were again ready to take action. More consumer-oriented legislation was passed than ever before, including the Securities Act of 1933 (which provided potential investors with protection against deceptions concerning new issues of corporate securities), the Federal Food, Drug, and Cosmetic Act of 1938 (which strengthened the Pure Food and Drug Act of 1906), and the Wheeler-Lea amendments to the Federal Trade Commission Act of 1914 (which extended "unfair methods of competition" to include deceptive acts or practices).[12] The Wheeler-Lea amendments eliminated the problems of the *Raladam* decision for the FTC.

Consumer Research and Consumers Union were born; Sears, Roebuck and Macy's tested products before selling them; *Good Housekeeping* checked products to ensure that advertising claims were accurate; the American Medical Association tested proprietary drugs; and the National Bureau of Standards tested products before government purchase.[13]

But the movement, which had lasted almost two decades, faltered again. Postwar recovery and the increasing affluence of the 1950s moved the consumer into a period of complacency.

In the 1960s, however, the movement again picked up steam in response to a number of influential underlying currents, including the following: (1) technology which produced products that were considerably less than 100 percent reliable; (2) a series of revelations about the ingredients used in frankfurters and hamburgers and about the condition of fisheries and our water supplies; (3) reports of corruption of public officials on an unprecedented scale; (4) soaring medical and dental costs; and (5) special tax privileges for the few.[14] These trends, combined with best-sellers such as John Kenneth Galbraith's *The Affluent Society*,[15] Rachel Carson's *Silent Spring*,[16] and Ralph Nader's *Unsafe at Any Speed*,[17] helped to produce the consumer movement of the '60s and '70s.

New consumer laws included the Fair Packaging and Labeling Act of 1965 (to regulate the packaging and labeling of consumer goods), the Child Safety Act of 1966 (to strengthen the Hazardous Substance Labeling Act of 1960 by preventing the marketing of potentially harmful toys), the Consumer Credit Protection Act of 1968 (to require disclosure of annual interest rates and other finance charges on consumer loans and credit buying, including revolving charge accounts), and the Federal Boat Safety Act of 1971 (to provide for a coordinated national boating safety program).[18]

The post of Special Assistant for Consumer Affairs was established under President Johnson, and Ralph Nader became institutionalized by establishing far-flung organizations throughout the country to deal with consumer matters. Housewives boycotted stores to protest high meat prices while other housewives formed Action for Children's Advertising, a potent lobbying group that is still attempting to correct abuses in advertising to children.

The Outlook for Consumerism

As we move through the '80s, how will consumerism fare? There is great divergency on this issue. Some negative views include a 1982 Harris poll which found a greater mistrust of consumer activists than in the 1970s. In 1977, 22 percent of the respondents had agreed with the statement that activists such as Ralph Nader were out of touch with consumer interests.[19] In the 1982 poll, the percentage in agreement had more than doubled, to 45 percent. This later Harris poll also found that respondents believed that consumerists "do not consider the cost of what they are asking for."[20]

Assael believes a major flaw in the consumer movement of the 1960s and 1970s was its failure to leave behind some sort of national consumer organization. Lacking such an organization, consumers have not been able to establish a major countervailing force to big business.[21] The implication of this statement may be that the consumer movement, as we have discussed it, cannot continue to leap from one issue to the next without losing some of its momentum. Only with an established intrastructure, like a national consumer organization, can the movement continue to move forward and prosper.

Bloom and Greyser have a somewhat different perspective:

Although it is in the mature stage of its life cycle, consumerism is not, we believe, in a declining or faltering stage. We reached this conclusion after considering the results of several recent public opinion surveys which point to continuing strong, though latent, public demand for actions that help consumers obtain a better deal. We also believe that certain aspects of consumerism—redress assistance, education, cooperative buying, and deregulation—are still well accepted, although some older offerings (such as consumer protection legislation) have fallen on hard times.

In sum, we foresee a quieter but still active consumer movement during the 1980s. We think the public will shift from its past role as largely cheering spectators to one of active participants. We envision participative consumerism a major characteristic of the marketplace.

The daily behavior of many people will be influenced by consumerist issues; we expect consumerism to entail a great deal of activity by people on their own—like consumer education, consumer information, redress assistance, cooperative buying, and home-grown products. On the other hand, we anticipate much less activity propelled by national organizations and their leaders.[22]

Returning to our original question—How will consumerism fare?—it appears that there is no definite prognosis. The consumer movement is a myriad of ideas and organizations. It ranges from national organizations to highly specialized locals. Some elements of the movement view the consumer as the "economic man" discussed in earlier chapters while other elements call for protection in the broadest sense. Some see the need for legislation while others call for more "individual consumerism" through education. Some areas will prosper while others will not, but the heyday of the movement is over for the moment.

SELF-REGULATORY
FORCES

Self-regulation is not new to the institution of advertising. During the last two decades of the 1800s, the *Ladies Home Journal* and *Good Housekeeping* developed advertising acceptance policies. In the early 1900s, the *Printers' Ink Model Statute* was developed and later became the model for many state advertising laws. During the 1920s, Better Business Bureaus were established to help deal with such practices as false comparisons, misleading statements, false claims as to quality, and "bait and switch" advertising.

Is self-regulation an admission that natural market forces are insufficient to regulate the marketplace or is it simply a reaction to increased concern on the part of consumerists and governmental agencies? Zanot provides a perspective:

Apparently self-regulation has been a response and a reply to forces impinging upon the trade from the outside. Self-regulation can be considered a reaction by the trade to downturns in the economy, criticism from the public or, especially, the threat of legislation. Although the altruistic motive of protecting consumers undoubtedly enters to some degree, the primary motive behind self-regulation is thought to be enlightened self-interest. Although this analysis does not permit tight cause-and-effect statements, it appears that the trade has used self-regulation to not only eradicate false and deceptive advertising but also to dampen public criticism and forestall government legislation.[23]

The National Advertising Division and the National Advertising Review Board

Whatever the reason for the establishment of self-regulatory mechanisms, it is still important to review the major ones and discuss their effectiveness. In 1971, the American Association of Advertising Agencies, the American Advertising Federation, the Association of National Advertisers, and the Council of Better Business Bureaus (CBBB) established the National Advertising Review Council, which in turn established two operating arms, the National Advertising Division (NAD) of the Council of Better Business Bureaus and the National Advertising Review Board (NARB). The chief purpose of the National Advertising Review Council is to seek the voluntary withdrawal of national advertising that professionals consider to be deceptive.

The NAD operates on a full-time basis and is staffed by people with backgrounds in advertising. It essentially receives complaints or questions about the truthfulness of national advertising from a variety of sources including competitors, consumers, and local Better Business Bureaus. The NAD also has its own monitoring system.

When a complaint is received, the NAD may contact the advertiser in question and request material to substantiate the claims made in the advertisement. If it finds the substantiation inadequate, it urges the advertiser to modify or withdraw the advertising. If a satisfactory resolution cannot be found by either the advertiser or the NAD, the case is referred to the NARB.

The NARB is composed of thirty representatives of national advertisers, ten from advertising agencies (plus ten alternates to avoid conflict of interest), and ten members of unrelated fields. This last component of the NARB group membership marks the first time in the history of self-regulation that non-industry individuals have been included.

When a case is referred to the NARB, five members are assigned to the case. If the final decision of these five members is not accepted by the advertiser (assuming it is a negative one from the advertiser's point of view) the NARB will refer the matter to the appropriate government agency. In addition to referring the case to more traditional legal channels, the board will make public the facts of the disputed case along with any statement the advertiser might wish to make. Tables 8-1 and 8-2 present data on the activity of the NAD and the NARB since their establishment in 1971.

It should be noted that since 1975 more than half of the cases brought before the NAD resulted in the advertising being modified or discontinued (the exception being 1977). Is the self-regulating mechanism performing adequately? Certainly, a large volume of cases have been brought before the NAD. Whether the advertisers or the self-regulatory process has "won" is at best only a value judgment. Given the pro-business mood in Washington and the more introverted consumerism of the '80s, will the self-regulatory mechanism continue to perform as it has? If Zanot's premise that self-regulation springs primarily from self-interest is accepted, the answer would be no.

The Children's Advertising Review Unit

In 1974, the NAD created the Children's Advertising Review Unit (CARU), which is funded by major children's advertisers. The CARU attempts to review advertising through the eyes of children, taking into account that they may lack the sophistication and understanding of adult audiences. The CARU tries to ensure that children's advertising is fair, with the word fair encompassing such issues as social values, product presentation, pressure of purchase, endorsements, safety, and premiums.[24]

Ads are evaluated against the CARU guidelines which were revised in 1983. The staff makes subjective judgments about ads, sometimes with the advice of the CBBB's legal staff. In addition seven academic advisors are occasionally consulted on matters relating to particular cases.

Armstrong made a rather complete review of the CARU activities from 1974 to 1982 and has drawn some interesting conclusions:

1. The caseload is small by any standard (an average of about 15 cases per year, and falling, as compared to about 175 cases per year for NAD). Though casework may provide input for the development and testing of the Unit's guidelines, this volume of cases is probably too small to enforce the guidelines effectively or to set meaningful precedents for improvement of advertising to children.
2. CARU casework appears to be largely inner-directed, even more so than NAD casework. Most is generated from internal monitoring. CARU has even less consumer input than NAD (14% vs. NAD's 22%) and is used much less by advertisers to resolve complaints against competition (3% vs. NAD's 38% in recent years).
3. The level of case activity appears to fluctuate substantially with external pressures in children's advertising. For example, efforts peaked in 1978-79 when the industry was threatened by the FTC trade regulation rule on children's advertising. When the threat had passed, the caseload decreased considerably.

TABLE 8-1
Source of Complaints Handled by the NAD, 1971-1984 (in Percentages)

SOURCE OF COMPLAINT[a]	1971	1972	1973	1974	1975	1976	1977	1978	1979	1980	1981	1982	1983	1984
NAD monitoring	10	10	51	40	35	52	56	48	34	45	43	39	37	31
Competitor challenges	2	6	8	11	27	25	21	36	39	37	35	39	42	45
Local BBB's[b]	53	20	15	22	16	10	11	12	9	12	12	10	11	10
Consumer complaints	9	25	14	13	15	10	9	2	16	6	8	9	5	9
Other[c]	26	39	12	14	7	3	3	2	2	—	2	3	5	5
	100%	100%	100%	100%	100%	100%	100%	100%	100%	100%	100%	100%	100%	100%

[a] Based on incoming cases; year 1982 forward based on published reports.
[b] Half of all BBB referrals are estimated to be consumer initiated.
[c] Includes organized consumer groups, professional or trade associations, federal and state regulatory agencies.

Source: National Advertising Division, 1985.

TABLE 8-2
Cases Closed by the NAD, 1971-1984

DISPOSITION OF CASE	MID-1971 THROUGH 1973	1974	1975	1976	1977	1978	1979	1980	1981	1982	1983	1984
Substantiated	191	75	72	67	94	64	63	57	68	61	46	22
Modified/discontinued	126	65	101	95	60	99	99	78	80	79	64	83
Referred to NARB	9	2	—	1	1	—	1	—	1	—	—	—
Suspended pending FTC litigation	—	—	—	—	—	—	—	—	1	—	—	—
Total	326	142	173	163	155	163	163	135	150	140	110	105

Source: National Advertising Division, 1985.

4. The development of a set of specific guidelines appears to have aided
    CARU in its casework. Comparison with NAD (which has no such
    guidelines) show that CARU had higher proportions of initial "unac-
    ceptable" decisions (71% vs. NAD's 16%) and fewer requests to sub-
    stantiate (22% vs. NAD's 82%). The Unit resolved more cases in its
    favor (37% vs. 31% for NAD) and received more "previously discon-
    tinued" responses (38% vs. 17%). These and other facts imply that the
    guidelines have resulted in better CARU case selection and propor-
    tionally greater effectiveness in removing potentially abusive ads.[25]

Armstrong feels that the CARU "is little more than a token effort by the
advertising industry. It is an organization with sweeping and impressive
mandate to assure truth, accuracy, and fairness and to develop precedents and advisories for the improvement of child-directed advertising
but with paltry resources with which to accomplish the mission. Given
the extent of its mandate, CARU is seriously undermanned and
under-funded."[26]

Armstrong's conclusions may be a bit harsh, but he does raise serious
concerns about this attempt at self-regulation within the advertising industry. Given the seriousness of the children's issue, it is important that
this form of advertising be monitored vigorously.

GOVERNMENTAL FORCES

Our focus in this discussion of government forces will be the federal
level. Although all states and some local jurisdictions attempt to deal
with advertising, their approaches are often so varied that it is impossible
to arrive at a common position regarding their efforts.

Before we begin a discussion of the formal regulatory process, it is
necessary to stress the importance of the "mood" of Washington in legislation and enforcement. The philosophy of the White House during any
given administration strongly influences what legislation will be passed
and what area of enforcement the Justice Department and the Federal
Trade Commission will concentrate on.

The mood of Washington under the Reagan administration is best
summarized in the president's 1982 economic report: "While regulation
is necessary to protect such vital areas as food, health, and safety, too
much unnecessary regulation simply adds to the costs of businesses and
consumers alike without commensurate benefits."[27] The Reagan administration has made clear its position that government regulation is justifiable only if it (1) produces benefits that outweigh the costs, and (2) is the
least expensive solution to the problem.[28]

As a result, regulatory agencies are being required to justify their actions with some type of cost-benefit analysis indicating the value of the
proposed regulation. As Assael has pointed out, this puts the burden of

proof on the agencies, "whereas in the 1970's the burden of proof was on industry to ensure consumer protection."[29]

The 1980s have also meant cutbacks in most consumer agencies. Concerning the agency we are most interested in, the Federal Trade Commission (FTC), the following has occurred:

1. Elimination of a proposed rule to ban certain advertising to children.
2. Elimination of industry-wide guidelines for advertising claims in the over-the-counter drug market.
3. Elimination of rules that would have required manufacturers to disclose nutritional information.
4. Elimination of a rule that would have added to advertising warnings now required on labels of antacid products.
5. Elimination of rules requiring disclosures within food ads making health and nutrition claims.[30]
6. Elimination of its ten-year-old case against the three leading cereal manufacturers in which the FTC claimed that the companies' advertising and marketing practices constitute "shared monopoly" resulting in higher prices.[31]

In addition, Congress passed the Federal Trade Improvement Act of 1980, which revised the manner in which the FTC could improve trade rules and regulations, provided for congressional review of the commission's actions, and removed "unfairness" as the basis for trade rules dealing with advertising.[32] Now deception had to be present to justify a new industry-wide trade rule or court litigation.

During the 1980s, the Reagan administration also appointed a new chairman of the FTC, James C. Miller III. Although Miller has recently left the FTC, some of his proposals for sweeping changes in governmental regulation of the institution of advertising are likely to remain. Miller's three main proposals are as follows:

1. ADVERTISING SUBSTANTIATION. Miller suggested its abandonment. As Miller stated, "There's no free lunch. When firms are required to go out and prepare these 'reasonable basis' reports, the costs are passed on to consumers."
2. ADVERTISING DECEPTION. Miller proposed changing the present criterion for deception—"having the tendency or capacity to deceive"—to a far more narrow set of requirements. The commission would now have to prove that "reasonable consumers" (with some exceptions for vulnerable groups) were misled. Deception must now be intended.
3. REDUCING THE FTC's AUTHORITY. Miller suggested reducing the FTC budget to create a "lean and mean" agency. He indicated he wanted the agency to go after "nuts and bolts" areas and not waste the taxpayers' money as it had done in the previously mentioned cereal

case, which had dragged on for ten years and cost the taxpayers over $30 million.[33]

Dramatic evidence of the altered mood of Washington under the Reagan administration can be found in a comparison of Miller's proposals with the following major policy decisions made by the FTC a decade earlier, during the early 1970s:

1. ADVERTISING SUBSTANTIATION. This program required advertisers to submit, on demand, data substantiating claims made regarding comparative aspects of price, safety, or performance.
2. CORRECTIVE ADVERTISING. This FTC strategy would require advertisers who have made deceptive or unfair claims to spend a certain amount of future advertising dollars to make statements to correct the deception. Listerine was required to spend $10 million to communicate the message, "Listerine will not help prevent colds or sore throats or lessen their severity."
3. UNFAIRNESS. The FTC contended that it was unfair for companies to make performance claims unless the company had adequately substantiated the claim before the advertising appeared. The main thrust of this policy was to shift the burden of proof of product effectiveness to the advertiser.
4. AFFIRMATIVE DISCLOSURE. This policy would require marketers and advertisers to inform potential customers of certain facts about the product or service offered. Ingredient listings and warnings would be included.

Although these policies established in the early 1970s are still "on the books," little action has been taken by the FTC in the last ten years to utilize them as regulatory tools. The future prospects for their utilization appear bleak, at least under the current FTC chairman and the administration in Washington.

MEDIA FORCES

In 1979, a civil antitrust suit was brought against the National Association of Broadcasters (NAB) charging that its television-code rules that regulate television advertising were anticompetitive and in restraint of trade. In 1982, a consent decree was signed by all parties which basically eliminated the NAB code. There are now no formal standards concerning:

1. The number of commercial minutes per hour.
2. The number of commercials per hour.
3. The number of consecutive commercials at each commercial interruption.

4. The number of products that can be promoted in a commercial last-
   ing less than 60 seconds.
5. The purchase of network time for liquor ads.
6. The actual consumption of beer or wine on television.[34]

There has already been some movement by the networks toward increasing the number of commercial minutes per hour along with some
discussion of selling fifteen-second spots for different products. Will this
breakdown of industry-wide codes bring more television clutter and
shorter, less informative advertisements? Will the networks respond to
the disappearance of the NAB code in a positive way or see it as an opportunity to increase their profitability?

Although not discussed openly, there is a general feeling that in making spot buys around the country there are less rigid standards for the
advertiser. Within individual networks, however, it appears that network review units have maintained a rather strict set of standards for
commercial acceptance.

It would appear that self-regulation on the media's part is in some
state of disarray. What future impact the media will have on the institution of advertising remains to be seen.

SUMMARY

Returning to the question at the beginning of the chapter—What forces
should be allowed to regulate the institution of advertising?—it is clear
that there will always be some combination of forces involved in regulation. The exact mix of these forces is dependent on the tenor of the times.
Since shifts in sociopolitical attitudes change the mix from decade to
decade, one probably should not expect to find a consistent stream and
heritage of regulation. A certain amount of instability in the marketplace
is inevitable for both advertisers and consumers.

The swing of the sociopolitical pendulum toward deregulation has
allowed natural market forces to dominate. Consumers are now viewed
as more capable of looking out for themselves than the government has
given them credit for. The market is viewed as a capable regulator, enabling sellers and buyers at different levels of market sophistication to
interact well.

Will this feeling about the marketplace spill over to the self-
regulatory mechanisms currently in place? Will the quieter, more individualistic consumerism of the 1980s find little need for concern about
the changes in the legal environment or the self-regulatory system? How
will the consumer fare in this environment? As discussed in Chapter 3,
depending on the sets of assumptions the reader makes about such fun-

damental matters as human nature, the proper role of the market, and the presence of government, the resultant feeling may be one of optimism or of pessimism.

Notes

1. William T. Kelley, ed., *New Consumerism: Selected Readings* (Columbus, Ohio: Grid, Inc., 1973), p. vi.
2. Ibid., p. iv.
3. Eugene R. Beem, "The Beginnings of the Consumer Movement," in *New Consumerism: Selected Readings*, ed. William T. Kelly (Columbus, Ohio: Grid, Inc., 1973), p. 13.
4. Upton Sinclair, *The Jungle* (New York: Viking Press, 1946); originally published in 1906).
5. Beem, op. cit., pp. 17-18.
6. Ibid., pp. 18-19.
7. Francis J. Charlton and William A. Fawcett, "The FTC and False Advertising," *Kansas Law Review*, vol. 17 (1969), p. 606.
8. *FTC vs. Raladam Co.*, 283 U.S. 643.
9. Stuart Chase and Frederick J. Schlink, *Your Money's Worth* (New York: Macmillan, 1927), p. 254.
10. Mary C. Phillips, *Skin Deep* (New York: Vanguard Press, 1934).
11. Frederick J. Schlink, *Eat, Drink and Be Wary* (New York: Covici-Friede Co., 1935).
12. Marshall C. Howard, *Legal Aspects of Marketing* (New York: McGraw-Hill Book Co., 1974), pp. 10-11.
13. Beem, op. cit. p. 28.
14. "MIN's Historical Perspective on Consumerism," *Media Industry News Letter*, May 11, 1972, p. 7.
15. John Kenneth Galbraith, *The Affluent Society* (Boston: Houghton Mifflin, 1958).
16. Rachel Carson, *Silent Spring* (Boston: Houghton Mifflin, 1962).
17. Ralph Nader, *Unsafe at Any Speed* (New York: Grossman, 1965).
18. Ralph M. Gaedeke and Warren W. Etcheson, *Consumerism Viewpoints from Business, Government, and the Public Interest* (San Francisco: Canfield Press, 1972), pp. 374-375.
19. "New Harris Consumer Study Causes Few Shocks in Adland," *Advertising Age*, May 30, 1977, p. 2.
20. *New York Times*, February 17, 1983, p. A-16.
21. Henry Assael, *Consumer Behavior and Marketing Action* (Boston: Kent Publishing Co., 1983), p. 622.
22. Paul N. Bloom and Stephen A. Greyser, "The Maturing of Consumerism," *Harvard Business Review*, November-December, 1981, p. 131.

23. Eric J. Zanot, "The National Advertising Review Board: Precedents, Premises, and Performance," doctoral dissertation, University of Illinois, College of Communication, 1977, pp. 62-63.

24. Gary M. Armstrong," An Evaluation of the Children's Advertising Review Unit," *Journal of Public Policy & Marketing* 3 (1984), p. 39.

25. Ibid., pp. 51-52.

26. Ibid., p. 53.

27. *New York Times*, January 21, 1983, p. A-16.

28. "Deregulation, A Fast Start for the Reagan Strategy," *Business Week*, March 9, 1981, p. 62.

29. Assael, op. cit., p. 628.

30. "Despite Antiregulatory Sentiment, Advertisers Still Must Battle Washington 'Policy Shapers,' " *Marketing News*, April 30, 1982, p. 1.

31. C. H. Sandage, Vernon Fryburger, and Kim Rotzoll, *Advertising Theory and Practice* (Homewood, Ill.: Richard D. Irwin, Inc., 1983), p. 483.

32. William H. Bolen, *Advertising* (New York: John Wiley & Sons, 1984), p. 59.

33. Sandage, op. cit., p. 483.

34. Bolen, op. cit., p. 76.

Chapter 9

Advertising
and Its
Ethical
Dimensions

A 1983 Gallup poll ranked people in the advertising business 24th out of 25 occupational groups in terms of honesty and ethical standards.[1] But perhaps those responding to the poll didn't really *know* any advertising people. Perhaps. But what, then, do we do with a 1977 study published in *Advertising Age* in which not one of the neighbors of advertising practitioners polled could "conceive of an advertising person whom they would designate as a solid citizen" or "honest" or "straightforward"?[2] Or practitioner Howard Gossage, elected to the Copywriters Hall of Fame: "To explain responsibility to advertising people is like trying to convince an eight-year-old that sexual intercourse is more fun than a chocolate ice cream cone."[3]

Not surprisingly, these and other reasonably consistent findings dismay many in the advertising business. They point to a host of guidelines, codes, self-regulatory bodies, and *pro bono publico* efforts such as the Advertising Council and its $600 million-plus effort on behalf of good causes. They contend (rightfully) that many of their colleagues are among the most socially concerned individuals they know, and that countless after-hours efforts on behalf of various community and special-interest causes benefit by their volunteered (but largely unrecognized) expertise.

AREAS OF INHERENT
ETHICAL ENCOUNTER

Why the conflicts, then? Perhaps most fundamentally, if we consider ethics the study of voluntary human conduct in the sense that it can be judged right or wrong in relation to determinative principles, there may simply be ethical strains which are endemic to the philosophy, structure, and practice of the advertising business. Some of the most arresting:

1. *Advertising operates from an essentially classical liberal ethic.* As we have seen, the premises of classical liberalism and their assumed operation in a complex socioeconomic system are today the stuff of conflict and ambiguity. A review of Chapter 3 will indicate how the assumptions one chooses to make about self-interest, the presumed rationality of individuals, the purging force of competition, etc., can result in very different views about whether the good of the whole is being served and, hence, whether the economy and advertising are or are not in need of regulation. Simply, those who operate from one set of premises may regard the actions of those endorsing another as unethical.

2. *The advertising message is inherently biased.* As Carey observed in his essay discussed in Chapter 4, advertising as a form of market information is a powerful concept. And when firms *in* the market—rather than the market *itself* through countless interpersonal transactions—began supplying the information, there were significant trade-offs in terms of message content and availability. Thus, it is presumed to be in the best interests of the advertiser to provide only that information most beneficial to the firm's interests, with the assumption that if these do not harmonize with the potential customer's interests, lack of patronage will result, and the invisible hand will work its way. But clearly critics find this idealism wanting in the face of their perception of deceptively incomplete messages that result, at best, in less than optimal market decisions and, at worst, in the adoption of decision-making criteria based on the trivial rather than the substantive.

3. *The advertising message is inherently persuasive.* Advertising, like other forms of special pleading, generally wants us to change. To change our minds, to change our behavior. And Americans have, throughout our history, had a love/hate relationship with those who make these attempts. From the drummers of the frontier to Willy Loman, televised evangelism, politicians on the stump, and the all-too-frequent pitches for the Ginzu knife sets of the world ("*Now*, how much would you pay for . . .") overt persuasion can be, by turns, captivating or revolting—with all the ethical confrontations that ensue.

4. *Advertising usually seeks out the individual.* Generally, with the exceptions of directories, catalogs, the Yellow Pages, and the like, advertising seeks us out rather than the other way around. This will, of course, raise questions of invasion of privacy, particularly in the broadcast media or those environments where we expect to be left alone and aren't—e.g., billboards, cinema advertising, T-shirts, hot-air balloons, scoreboards, toilet stalls, ski-lift towers, parking meters, the back seats of taxis, etc. Some of this seeking is welcome from the outset, some merely tolerated, some actively avoided. In the latter conditions the questions raised by

former practitioner Jerry Mander are illustrative: "Why do we tolerate this? What right do advertisers have to treat us this way?"[4]

5. *Advertising is a frequent third party with the mass media.* Since the early years of this century in print, and since the '20s and '50s on radio and television respectively, advertising has become an important third party in the basic relationship between publisher/reader and broadcaster/listener-viewer. Much good can be seen to come from this, but many inherent problems as well, as Chapter 7 suggests. If the mass media of this country consider their primary role to be the gathering of markets to sell to advertisers, then the configuration and, indeed, life or death of these vehicles will be determined primarily by market-delivery criteria and only secondarily by the satisfaction that the reader/listener/viewer derives from the non-advertising content of the media vehicle. The ethical perils are apparent.

6. *The major form of advertising agency compensation places strains on the possibility of a truly professional relationship.* The advertising agency commission system, born in the last century when early advertising agents served as space brokers, continues to be the standard against which financial arrangements between agency and client are established. At its simplest level, the advertising agency is paid on the basis of how much of the advertiser's money is spent on the purchase of advertising time and space in the mass media. Thus, the agency finds itself in the position of having its *own* financial well-being linked with growing media expenditures for its clients. This may or may not be related to the financial well-being of the *client*, but given the difficulty in determining a cause-and-effect relationship between advertising and sales, the linkage is likely to remain obscure. Not at all obscure are the ethical consequences.

7. *Underlying many of the preceding is the uncertainty inherent in the advertising process.* If, as we have discussed frequently throughout this book, and explicitly in Chapter 1, even the most well-intentioned advertisers have a difficult time determining the effectiveness of their often expensive advertising efforts, it's hardly surprising that there are disagreements about what, if anything, is being done to whom for whose ultimate benefit. The current turmoil about the effects of the advertising of alcoholic beverages on television and advertising directed to children are two cases in point among many.

QUALIFICATIONS BY ADVERTISING TYPES

We have repeatedly made the point that it is not productive to generalize about advertising. Thus in any discussion of advertising ethics it is important to be conscious of possible differences between, say, national consumer advertising, retail advertising, business advertising, advertising by individuals, etc. Based on the seven factors just discussed, then, are there likely to be greater ethical strains in some areas of advertising practice than in others? Perhaps.

First, it can be contended that *all* advertisers operate from at least implicit assumptions about the inherent justice of a system that allows them—indeed encourages them—to seek their self-interest. All also generally share the assumption that the result of these efforts of persuasion will be of general benefit to seller and buyer alike. Thus ethical disagreements arising from the clash between these assumptions and other, quite different sets of assumptions are inevitable, regardless of advertising form.

Advertising by its nature is biased, yet the ethical *consequences* may seem different by type. In general, one-sided information may seem more problematic when the recipient utilizes few other sources before arriving at a decision to act. (See Chapter 6.) An individual choosing between brands of a household item is far more likely to "take advertising's word for it" than is a purchasing agent for an automobile company considering who should be chosen as the next supplier of degreasing solvent. Also, retailers may boast, but their claims are easily tested by experience—either our own or that of people we know. Experience can be a great leveler with consumer goods advertising as well, but it's simply more difficult to "know" whether the brand-name aspirin does indeed "work wonders," or whether the fact that a beer is "fire-brewed" should be at all important to us. And so on.

All advertising attempts to persuade. Yet important questions are "How?" and "About what?" It may be hypothesized that the more closely the subject matter of the advertisement meshes with the interest of the individual, the more the persuasion will be tolerated, or even welcomed. Thus, the more specialized the media, the more specialized the advertising, and, potentially, the fewer the ethical concerns about attempts to persuade. Again we return to national consumer goods advertising. Compare:

The seven deadly sins	and	The seven cardinal virtues
Greed		Wisdom
Lust		Justice
Sloth		Temperance
Pride		Courage
Envy		Faith
Gluttony		Hope
Anger		Love

Critics would contend that advertisers are far more likely to use appeals to the first than to the second, and consumer goods advertisers are far more likely to be so charged. (This is, it can be contended, the base line of the oft-heard contention that advertising causes us to buy things we don't want or need, thereby feeding the presumed darker side of human nature.) Yet supporters of advertising may contend, in sound pluralistic argumentation, that there are other institutions (e.g., churches, schools, etc.) attending to many of the cardinal virtues, and if advertising does indeed espouse their counterparts, it is only one voice among many to which the individual may or may not attend. Advertising, John O'Toole asserts in a representative statement, is "not journalism or education and cannot be judged on the basis of objectivity and exhaustive, in-depth treatment."[5] Obviously, critics would dissent.

The ethical dimensions of the role of advertising as a benefactor/tyrant in relation to the mass media seem relatively pervasive. Although much public criticism is, predictably, directed toward television and the presumed degrading effect that advertising-sensitive programming causes, abuses in magazines, newspapers, trade papers, the business press, etc., are equally apparent to all choosing to look. Any time, it may be hypothesized, that the media need advertisers more than the advertisers need particular media vehicles, influence pandering and power plays are virtually inevitable.

The ethical pressures brought by the agency commission system seem more likely to be accentuated with large-budget consumer goods accounts, particularly those using television. Retailers do not commonly use agencies, nor do most newspapers usually grant agency commissions for local accounts. Business advertisers frequently rely on other financial arrangements with their agencies (e.g., fees) because the cost of media space in business publications is often not high enough to generate satisfactory commissions for the acting agency.

Again, although advertising practice is generally underlaid with the uncertainty of the process, it seems particularly acute at the national advertiser level because the indirect effect on sales through retail outlets at some later time makes the task of untangling the other possible influential variables particularly vexing. Retailers can often feel comfortable using increases in store traffic or sales as rough indexes of their advertising efforts, while business advertising is often used to generate leads for the personal sales force, thus providing direct response through reply cards, toll-free telephone numbers, etc.

Like any other complex institution, then, advertising holds within its operating norms certain *fundamental* relationships and commonly accepted modes of behavior that can have important ethical consequences, *depending upon what value system is applied to the evaluation.* For example, using classical liberal considerations, some "problems" simply don't arise because they are assumed to be resolved by the normal workings of the market system. Thus, advertising practitioners who might be considered amoral by "social responsibility" standards could in fact be relying upon the assumed morality of the market system with its implicit checks and balances. Equally apparent, however, is the observation that the discussed areas do spawn ethical encounters, and, further, that these are far more likely to be accentuated with some types of advertising than with others, particularly national consumer goods advertising, particularly on television. This is, we feel, a necessary backdrop for further exploration.

SEVERAL CENTRAL ETHICAL AREAS

A 1980 study[6] of advertising agency practitioners (those most likely to be working with national consumer goods products, the arguable focal point for ethical concerns in advertising) asked practitioners if they encountered ethical decisions (undefined) in their day-to-day work. Most responded that they did, although copywriters and art directors were least likely to agree. The classical liberal (invisible hand) theme of many of those suggesting that they did *not* is captured in this response:

- Any action I would regard as non-ethical, I would also view as inexpedient at the more pragmatic level. This includes actions toward the consumer, or a business company or individual. Since the pragmatic is an earlier more immediate consideration and the check operates in an ethical manner, I do not believe that an ethical decision needs to be made.

  It has been said that advertising forces the consumers to buy products they don't need, cannot afford or are detrimental to their health. I don't agree. Advertising cannot twist the consumer's arm. It simply supplies information and the consumer makes the buying decision from the information obtained. I tend to look at the good advertising does. It forces product competition, thereby encouraging higher quality products.

In general, two major areas of ethical concern arose from the responses to the study: the advertising message and agency/client relationships.

THE ADVERTISING MESSAGE. Many respondents focused on the question of *what should be advertised.* For example:

- Involvement in advertising products which may offer no real value to consumers and in some cases may even prove harmful (e.g., fruit drinks/ sodas with high levels of sugar, dyes, etc.). I do not think I could ever work on a cigarette brand (though my agency does)—and I myself do smoke. Yet I do feel it's wrong to promote smoking.
- Products which have been developed with no real improvement in which we are requested to manufacture excitement. In some cases the products designed for specific uses are undifferentiable, so again, no real end benefit to a consumer. In cases such as these, I point out the problem and press for real product improvement or differentiation, because I per-

sonally cannot recommend a product I will not use myself or have no faith in.

Given the subject area of the advertisement, there were also ample concerns about the complexities in the *crafting of the message*:

- If I decide the best way to sell breakfast cereal to tots is to accuse parents of mistreating their offspring (obliquely, of course) via malnourishment, this avenue is open to me. Only governing factors are client sensitivity and legal misrepresentations. Likewise, I can (if not restricted) appeal to uneducated consumers with possible unnecessary product appeals. (Uneducated, lower-income consumers, for example, are "easy sales" for laxatives, etc.)

- I have not decided whether "puffery" is unethical. Yet I do feel that if an advertiser has to tell the whole truth he may not as well advertise—there'd be no competitive advantage since most products are parity—with only minor grades of differences.

- We want to show our product in the best light. But how far do we go in making our product look good—or the competition look bad—before we are being unfair, dishonest, and are misleading the public? There are ways to word a claim that are perfectly "legal," but leave a stronger impression on the viewer. We carefully pick out the best potato chips to make an attractive-looking bowl. We throw away the broken discolored ones. We carefully dirty clothes in dirt that looks bad but can be removed by our detergent easily. Etc.

An intriguing dimension, discussed by many respondents, dealt with the question of *where the ethical decision making should properly occur.* Some saw it as residing *outside* the individual:

- Legal substantiation required by client, advertising agency and TV networks are so exhaustive as to not permit latitude for individual decision-making on ethical matters.

Still others reacted to the ambiguities of the advertising craft by suggesting that no matter how tight the external net, individual responsibility could not be abdicated:

- One situation involving ethical decisions: that in which there is an opportunity to use an advertising claim which, while factually true, is essentially misleading. This has not been influenced by the increased attention being paid to advertising by the FTC and other "watchdogs," since these groups are primarily interested in legalisms and factual substantiation for claims. "Truth" and "honesty" in advertising are two different things, and the latter is still primarily the ethical responsibility of individuals within the profession. These situations arise once or twice a year.

THE AGENCY/CLIENT RELATIONSHIP. As an organization offering a series of services around a product (the advertisement) whose exact effects are difficult to determine, the advertising agency encounters predictably complex, and ethically laden, situations.

One of the most fundamental of these is the meshing of self-interests on the part of the agency and the client. This is, as we have discussed, made particularly murky by the financial underpinning of the commission system, but there are other dimensions as well:

- Situations in which a marketing or advertising recommendation is called for which is in the best interests of the client, but not the agency. For example, a recommendation to replace a major ad campaign can mean loss of prestige and great expense for the agency. Likewise, recommendation to shift part of the marketing budget from advertising to promotion usually means lost income for the agency: these situations occur frequently.

Predictably there are difficulties in assigning financial values to advertising's stock-in-trade—the time and ideas of individuals. If, as Fairfax Cone is supposed to have said, an advertising agency's inventory "goes down the elevator every night," it sets the tone for inevitable differences of opinion among those individuals and those whose interests they presumably serve:

- Probably they [conflicts] arise most often over billing matters, and in making decisions that involve the risk of compromising the quality of service. There are natural conflicts among maintaining profitability, quality of service and completing work at a price that is attractive and affordable to the client. The severity of the conflict and number of times it becomes manifest depends a great deal on the client. E.g., if the client has little faith in research and pressures to reduce costs in that area, do you push on a recommendation for an expensive research project at the risk of upsetting (or even losing) a client although that particular piece of research seems necessary?

Finally, the agency practitioners responding to the survey touched upon another troublesome area—that of confidentiality. Employees of advertising agencies learn a great deal about the workings and plans of firms. That information is not without its value:

- In my opinion, businessmen are confronted with considerably more ethical decisions in the course of their careers than they would care to admit. I believe the most prevalent cases involve obtaining confidential information. Knowing what your competitor plans to do before he does it is a tremendous advantage, and obtaining such information any way you can get it without getting caught is becoming an accepted business practice.

These responses are certainly representative of many of the ongoing ethical arguments in advertising practice, particularly on the level of major national consumer goods advertisers. What ethical perspectives are in use, and with what consequences?

RELEVANT ETHICAL
SYSTEMS

A reading of the literature on ethics in advertising—including accusations by critics and assertions by practitioners—as well as frequent encounters with those working in the business generally reveal two predominant operating ethical systems:

1. *An "outside" system, relying upon codes, guidelines, formal regulations, etc.* Many advertising and media organizations have developed standards by which to assess advertising beyond the level of pure expediency.[7] Some are obviously more meaningful than others. It is of interest to note that when the long-standing code of the National Association of Broadcasters was set aside, the television networks incorporated many of its provisions. Yet that still left many independent stations without an overarching framework for clear yes/no decisions. And some involved in the network-clearance process have reported that they are noticing a new boldness in relation to the type of advertising that advertisers and agencies are now submitting for clearance. This is, of course, not unrelated to the general deregulatory climate encouraged by the Reagan administration.

The advertising business has been able to point with singular pride to the National Advertising Review Board mechanism, a complex self-regulatory body linked with the National Council of Better Business Bureaus. Since its inception in 1971, the NARB has been responsible for the most serious and efficient of advertising's not infrequent self-regulatory efforts.[8] Today it not only serves as an instigator and investigator of complaints dealing with alleged cases of deception and the like, but also assumes a normative posture with published guidelines on subjects such as the role of women in advertisements, advertising to children, etc.

And there is, of course, always the presence of the Federal Trade Commission and other relevant federal, state, and local government bodies. Their roles, and their effectiveness, vary greatly in accordance with prevailing political philosophies and whether any particular areas are highlighted by special interest groups (e.g., advertising to children, advertising of alcoholic beverages, stereotypes of women, minorities, the elderly, etc.). In any event their roles are often *post hoc* rather than normative.

But, as we have seen from statements of practitioners, all these "external" nets may be very porous indeed, sometimes because of philosophical commitment (e.g., a laissez-faire market policy) and sometimes because of the ingenuity of the perpetrators of ethical abuse.

2. *A personal system, commonly based on the standard of immediate consequences.* The classical liberal world view encourages short-run

(self-interested) thinking with the assumption that the long-run consequences of individual actions will be beneficial to the whole. It is not surprising, then, that evidence suggests that advertising practitioners commonly tend to base their ethical decisions on their assessment of the immediate effect of their actions on the parties most readily definable—e.g., the client, other members of the firm, etc.—and, implicitly, on the generalized receivers of the advertising message.

This can be seen as a version of utilitarianism, a major ethical system developed by British philosophers Jeremy Bentham and John Stuart Mill with its major premise, "Seek the greatest good for the greatest number."[9] Again, it can be seen as resting on a view of the market system in which advertisers contend that it is reasonable for them to pursue their narrow self-interest because others are doing the same, and, more broadly, that the purging effects of individual rationality and competition will assure an outcome beneficial to all who are involved in the process, at least in the long run. Given the complexity of the business it is not, at least on the surface, an inappropriate ethical framework. As Christians observed:

> First-class moral philosophers to the present choose utilitarianism as the best ethical system for complex situations in which there are a host of alternatives.[10]

There is, however, a clear dilemma here. If concern with the advertising message is the significant focal point in advertising's ethical arena—which it seems to be, and arguably *should* be—the *audience* must be of central concern. And, since even the most well-intentioned advertiser is more often than not unsure of what impact, if any, his or her firm's advertising will have on audience members, the uncertainty of outcome blunts utilitarianism's crucial assumption—a weighing of outcomes in terms of the greatest good for the greatest number beyond the more easily assessed impact on client, employees, etc.

Is the greatest good for the greatest number served by advertising to children? The "greatest number" would certainly be the children who receive the advertising. How, then, does one ascertain what good, if any, will ensue? Good for the children? Good for their parents? What about the trade-offs—the interruption of television programs with advertising messages, or the fact that the programs would probably not exist in the first place if it were not *for* the messages? Will the greatest good of the audience be served if they are not aware of all the relevant information about the product or service advertised? If the omnipresence of advertising overwhelms understanding of *all* the options available to them, *including not acting at all?*[11]

In short, whenever the potential audience of the advertising message is brought into the ethical model, utilitarianism falters. The critics, meanwhile, can feel quite comfortable in leveling charges—some profound, some absurd—concerning *their* interpretations of the *same* advertising activities based on largely neo-liberal assumptions.

Consider, then, that these are advertising's major areas of critical confrontation:

- Who should, and should not, be advertised to?
- What should, and should not, be advertised?
- What should, and should not, be the content of the advertising message?
- What should, and should not, be the symbolic tone of the advertising message?
- What should, and should not, be the relationship between advertising and the mass media?
- What should, and should not, be advertising's conscious obligation to society?

And, because of advertising's inherent ambiguity, it can be contended that these issues are more likely to be debated (implicitly or explicitly) with ethical rather than empirical criteria. Yet the dominant ethical system in use in the business is to a great extent dysfunctional *because* of that ambiguity.

An initial response is to suggest a reliance on some of the "external" standards discussed earlier. For if short-range self-interest is likely to dominate in personal ethical systems based largely on a utilitarianism weakened by the inherent difficulties in assessing audience outcomes, then external frameworks seem the only reasonable option.

But regulatory activities within the business will be reluctant to curb the inherent self-interest built into advertising's essentially classical liberal rationale in any fundamental way, relying instead on the provision of normative standards only in those areas of topical interest spotlighted by pressure groups—to date, the effect of advertising on children, the depiction of women in television ads, etc. And, even assuming a swing of the governmental pendulum toward a political climate more tolerant of regulation, government regulatory activity frequently tends to be on a case-by-case basis, with a reluctance to set business-wide standards in a society still honoring pluralism.

Thus, unless advertising is to become quite a different institution from the one we have encountered in its American history, there is no compelling reason to assume that advertising's ethical performance will become more credible, at least by its critics' standards. Advertising's areas of inherent ethical encounter are part of its institutional milieu. So, then, will be its ongoing controversies.

SUMMARY

Advertising and its practitioners are constantly savaged by critics who seek higher ethical standards in the philosophy and practice of the business. This is a particularly thorny issue because advertising, as normally practiced, seems to be on a collision course with ethical frameworks operating on other than classical liberal premises. Areas of inherent ethical encounter are heightened by:

- Advertising operating from a classical liberal ethic.
- The inherent bias of the advertising message.
- The persuasive intent of the advertising message.
- Advertising seeking out the individual.
- Advertising as a third party with the mass media.
- The agency commission system with its inherent conflicts of interest.
- The underlying uncertainty of the advertising process.

Although these factors are characteristic of all advertising practice, they seem particularly acute in the advertising of consumer goods and services by producers.

Practitioners generally regard the major areas of ethical concern as the advertising message and agency/client relations, with two predominant ethical systems: (a) a reliance on various external forces such as codes, guidelines, and formal regulations, and (b) a utilitarian (greatest good for the greatest number) personal system that seems thwarted by the difficulty in assessing advertising's possible effects on the potential receivers of the advertising message.

Given the nature of the business, and the endemic shortcomings in both of these operational ethical systems, advertising's ethical performance and reputation are unlikely to improve.

Notes

1. See John O'Toole, "Craft or Con?," *Madison Avenue*, August, 1984, p. 33.
2. *Advertising Age*, three-part series beginning vol. 48, no. 48 (November 28, 1977), p. 37.
3. Warren Hinckle, *If You Have a Lemon, Make Lemonade* (New York: G. P. Putnam's Sons, 1973), p. 353 ff.
4. Jerry Mander, "Four Arguments for the Elimination of Advertising," in *Advertising and the Public*, ed. Kim B. Rotzoll (Urbana: University of Illinois, Department of Advertising, 1980), p. 21.
5. John O'Toole, *The Trouble with Advertising* (New York: Chelsea House, 1981), p. 24.
6. Kim B. Rotzoll and Clifford G. Christians, "Advertising Agency Practitioners' Perceptions of Ethical Decisions," *Journalism Quarterly*, Autumn, 1980, pp. 425-431.
7. See Priscilla A. Labarbera, "Analyzing and Advancing the State of the Art of Advertising Self-Regulation," *Journal of Advertising*, vol. 9, no. 4 (1980), pp. 34-35.
8. See Eric G. Zanot, "A Review of Eight Years of NARB Casework," *Journal of Advertising*, vol. 9, no. 4 (1980), p. 20.

9. See Clifford G. Christians, Kim B. Rotzoll, and Mark Fackler, *Media Ethics* (New York: Longman, 1983), Introduction.
10. Rotzoll and Christians, op. cit., p. 430.
11. For an elaborated discussion of these and other points see Christians, Rotzoll, and Fackler, op. cit., ch. 6-10.

Afterword

In 1958 a perfectly wonderful book was published called *Madison Avenue, U.S.A.* Among his hundreds of interviews with the leading lights of advertising practice, journalist Martin Mayer held a session with J. Walter Thompson's legendary James Webb Young. Mayer recounts:

> Early in 1956, *Fortune* magazine sent a girl researcher up to see Jim Young at the Thompson company. . . . "She wanted to know about all the changes in the advertising business in the last twenty-five years," Young says. "When I told her there hadn't been any, she nearly fell off her chair. But it's true."[1]

This is a useful perspective to begin this tentative exploration of advertising's future with which we close the book. For, as we have argued elsewhere,[2] it can be contended that advertising's basic institutional forms were in place prior to 1915—i.e., the relationships between advertisers, agencies, and media; the agency commission system; the dependence of the media on advertising revenue; criticism and reform. Thus it is not surprising to find that two recent crystal-ball treatments of advertising by prominent practitioners give the distinct impression that the advertising of the future will be much like the advertising of the present—only more so.[3]

Specifically, the dominant word is specialization. There is agreement that increasingly "narrow" media forms—e.g., cable television, specialized magazines, various forms of direct marketing—will enable marketers to direct their advertising to the individuals who are most likely to be interested in the products or services (some estimate that 75 percent of the consumer sector will be dominated by services). This trend has at least the potential of lowering advertising's irritation factor, caused pre-

dominantly by involuntary exposure to the advertising of personally ir-
relevant products and services. But there is also agreement that there will
be *more* advertising, perhaps twice as much, caused primarily by shorter
television commercials, but also by expansion to other media forms—
e.g., cinema advertising. Thus, although the irritation level may be low-
ered as a result of greater efficiency in the advertiser/prospect/medium
mix, it may be raised by relentless, frequently involuntary, exposure to
special pleading.

It is clear that advertising, to one degree or another, reflects changes
in its culture. (This is not to dismiss the argument that advertising may
be a shaper of some of those changes, but advertising, like any other en-
during institution of a society, must remain linked to the central ideas—
i.e., Hamilton's "common sense"—shared by the constituencies to which
it relates.) Some of the forces *outside* the direct control of business, with
the potential to shape future advertising thought and practice, include
the following:

POPULATION FACTORS. By the turn of the century the much-
discussed "baby boomers" will be between their mid-30s and early 50s,
with predictable effects upon institutions. This is a group much sought
after by marketers because of their sheer numbers and overall affluence,
and they will clearly continue to influence the subjects and tone of advertising messages.

The growth of the Hispanic and non-white sectors of the population
will continue, with more advertising attention directed toward their
consumption potentials. A related factor is the presence of so-called
functional illiteracy, now estimated at close to 50 percent for each group.
Aside from the ominous strains on the social fabric, this will clearly influence such advertising-related factors as media selection.

It has been estimated that in the relatively near future 75 percent of
women may be in the work force, possibly reinforcing the trend toward
smaller families and accentuating advertisers' attempts to reach this important population segment.

Finally, it is reasonable to expect the average life span to lengthen,
through medical advances, better nutritional and exercise habits, and the
growth of health maintenance organizations (HMOs) promoting preven-
tive medicine and good health care practices.

TECHNOLOGICAL CHANGES. Innovations, of course, do not arrive
at fixed intervals. Even when potential is present, a host of economic,
political, or cultural factors may keep an invention from being fully developed. (If much of the futurist literature of the '40s was to be believed we
would now all be commuting by personal autogiros and living in fully
robotized homes.)

What seems safe at this juncture is to project a twenty-first century
strongly infused with microcircuitry, thus facilitating communication

and altering the workplace of home and factory. For better or for worse, this will presumably enable more personalized persuasion appeals. Also, the potential liberation from some of the rigors of the workplace will provide opportunities for an even more significant marketing emphasis on products and services for leisure time.

REGULATORY CLIMATE. As we have seen, there have been three rather clearly defined periods of intense regulatory activity in relation to advertising: the first two decades of the century; the 1930s; the late 1960s through the late 1970s. As the regulatory hand is lightened, excesses eventually emerge, thus leading to a new cycle of restriction. Currently the Reagan administration's laissez-faire economic philosophies support deregulatory practices. Yet, as history would indicate, there is every reason to expect a future tightening of the reins. At the moment this seems particularly likely in the areas of special audiences (particularly children) and the potential for abuse with unregulated cable systems. The possibilities of abuses in ever more personalized direct marketing efforts are also apparent.

GLOBAL IMPERATIVES. The notion of Spaceship Earth is not as fashionable now as it was 20 years ago. Yet, as we will shortly detail in another context, the specters of overpopulation, poverty, hunger, and pollution are present for all wishing to look. These landscapes can give pause to individuals pondering the allocation of planetary resources by market mechanisms that at times seem deadened to the imbalances between the haves and have-nots. The advertising business is not insensitive to these issues, and there is much good work done at the advertiser, agency, and media levels. Yet these offerings are minuscule in relation to the priorities of consumption. One may pause to realize that there is now close to $2 billion spent advertising and promoting cigarettes in this country, and speculate as to what good might ensue if the same amount were spent to address staggering concerns of famine in many parts of the world, nagging us to be more humanitarian as it now urges to be selfish.

"WORLD VIEW." Certainly, as IDEAS ⟶ INSTITUTIONS, it is clear that advertising achieves full flower as an institution under idea systems encompassing such assumptions about "human nature" as the positive values of self-interest, competition, and the belief that the private pursuit of profit will ultimately lead to societal gain. Should we change these ideas, the expectations and tolerations of advertising will change apace. Recent history would suggest an eventual swing of the pendulum back toward ideas more compatible with the modern liberal agenda and its philosophical thrust of social responsibility. In this case advertising would adapt, albeit in a somewhat more regulated state. Yet there is the possibility that what we are currently witnessing in the Reagan years is a true watershed—a reaffirmation of traditional classical liberal, free enterprise, individualistic values that may serve as the idea model for years to come, as the New Deal did for forty years and more. In either case, advertising seems destined to flourish, as both systems still rely heavily on our continuing ethic of private consumption.

In many ways, the heart of this issue is the individual as a decision maker. For, as we have seen, advertising flourishes in economic systems that allow considerable latitude for individuals to make their own decisions. Thus, although advertising can be logically associated with the market and capitalism, it can also exist in various mixed economies, such as those of Europe, the Middle East, and Japan, as long as individual decision making is encouraged, or at least tolerated.

The broadest question, then, is likely to be, To what extent can societies through the last quarter of this century and beyond continue to allow individual decision making instead of some type of national economic planning? Matters such as these will put the question to a test:

Energy. The world has finite natural energy resources. And there is an enormous gap between the use of those limited resources in the "have" versus the "have-not" countries. Can we allow individuals to continue to call their own energy shots through their purchases, or will elimination, or at least curtailment, of opportunities be necessary?

Ecology. Can we survive as a living planet? Again, can we continue to allow individual consumption, even though the end result may be a depletion of our precious ecosystem?

Poverty/Hunger. A relatively small percentage of this planet's population is well-off, while a proportion teeters at or near the brink of life. Can we continue to live with this staggering inequality? If not, what can be done, and how might market systems—based on individual self-interest—be affected?

In a very fundamental sense, the answers to these and related questions will determine the *presence* of advertising in the remaining years of this century and beyond.

As for its *impact*, that, of course, will continue to be the stuff of debate, in no small part because of differing assumptions about self-interest, rationality, competition, the state of the economy, and the proper role of regulation, as developed in Chapter 3. It is of interest to note that the historian Fox has concluded that advertising has *passed* its peak of institutional influence which, he asserts, it reached in the 1920s:

> Increasingly regulated on one side and increasingly scorned or ignored by consumers on the other, advertising has been shooting smaller weapons at a more garrisoned target. Along with most other contemporary institutions, advertising now has trouble finding anybody to believe it.[4]

Of course we can go back to Schudson's perspective of capitalist realism (Chapter 4) and its understanding that advertising does not *need* to be believed in order to effectively introduce and reinforce a pervasive value system.

On reflection, then, a realistic assessment of advertising in society, now, or in at least the foreseeable future, should require at least the following directives:

- What type of advertising is under consideration?
- What are the issues involved concerning that type?
- What are the essential assumptions about human nature, the relationship between the individual and the society, etc., that are held by the contending positions?
- Which set of assumptions, or what combination, do *you* find compatible?

For a host of reasons that we hope we have made clear, advertising seems destined to remain ambiguous, structured by its own internal complexities and the interests and passions of those observing it.

Daniel Boorstin once observed, "If we consider democracy as a set of institutions which aim to make everything available to anybody, it would not be an overstatement to describe advertising as the characteristic rhetoric of democracy."[5] It is our hope that these chapters have provided you with some perspectives, an array of analytic tools, to come to understand that rhetoric better.

There is an ancient Chinese curse that charges, "May you live in interesting times." The times for advertising, it seems, will *always* be interesting. And therein lies the curse . . . and the promise.

Notes

1. Martin Mayer, *Madison Avenue, U.S.A.* (New York: Harper & Brothers, 1958), p. 21.
2. Charles H. Sandage, Vernon Fryburger and Kim B. Rotzoll, *Advertising Theory and Practice*, 11th ed. (Homewood, Ill.: Richard D. Irwin, Inc., 1983), ch. 2.
3. "Advertising in the Year 2000: Tailoring Messages and Multiplying Media Outlets," *AAAA Newsletter* (New York: American Association of Advertising Agencies, December, 1984). The general thrust of this material is also found in Kim B. Rotzoll, "The Now and Future Advertising Education," *Journalism Educator*, Fall, 1985.
4. Stephen Fox, *The Mirror Makers* (New York: William Morrow and Co., 1984), p. 380.
5. Daniel G. Boorstin, "Advertising and American Civilization," in *Advertising and Society*, ed. Yale Brozen (New York: New York University Press, 1974), pp. 11-12.